I0469274

LEARNING
THE ART OF
CUSTOMER SERVICE

Gaining Lasting Loyalty—Aiming Sustained Profitability

The author started his career in the customer service industry in 2003 and has served some of the *Fortune 500* companies. After joining Convergys Corporation, he trained *Customer Service Professionals* to support *former* AT&T Wireless customers. Later, Cingular Wireless LLC, a joint venture between SBC Communications and BellSouth, acquired AT&T Wireless, forming the *new* Cingular Wireless; and finally, SBC acquired the *original* AT&T and re-branded all the lines of businesses including the wireless sector as AT&T; the author remained part of all the various transitions, serving the client in the capacity of training and development and preparing the customer service to meet the challenges that come with mergers and acquisitions—striving to keep the customer base loyal and the conversion period transparent without impacting the quality of the service. He left the wireless industry to instruct *Customer Service Professionals* to support Nissan USA and Nissan Canada consumers upon joining Aditya Birla Minacs. After serving the auto division for a time, he went back to the wireless business, this time preparing *Customer Service Professionals* to serve Sprint Nextel. In the private sector (ConAgra Foods Inc., Toyota Motor Sales, U.S.A., Inc.) he has also been part of the Information Technology to customize and support Enterprise Resource Planning (ERP) software. In the public sector (County of Simcoe) he has delivered training to various departments including Customer Service, Tourism, Museum, Social & Community Services, Economic Development, Long Term Care, and Libraries, to name a few. He is a graduate of University of Nebraska at Kearney and holds a Master's degree from Bellevue University. The author has enjoyed the privilege of being a member of both the *American Society of Training and Development* (ASTD) and the *Canadian Society of Training and Development* (CSTD).

Names of the **thought leaders** quoted in this book:

Adam Hochschild

Alan Weiss

Albert Einstein

Azim Premji

Bill Gates

Damon Richards

David Yu

Donald Porter

Doug Smith

Doug Warner

Edwards Deming

Gandhi

Ileana Kane

James Thurber

Jeff Bezos

Jerry Gregoire

Jerry Yang

Jimmy Carter

John Ilhan

John Russell

Joy Page

Kevin Stirtz

Leon Gorman

Lou Holtz

Ludwig Wittgenstein

Martin Oliver

Nelson Boswell

Nigel Sanders

Phillip Stranhope

Robert McCloskey

Roger Staubach

Rose Kennedy

Ross Perot

Sally Gronow

Sam Walton

Tony Allesandra

Voltaire

Warren Buffett

Zig Ziglar

LEARNING THE ART OF CUSTOMER SERVICE

Gaining Lasting Loyalty—Aiming Sustained Profitability

F. H. Zuberi

Copyright ©2013 by F. H. Zuberi

All rights reserved.

No part of this book may be reproduced or transmitted in any form or by any means now
known or to be invented, electronic or mechanical, including photocopying, recording, or
by any information storage or retrieval system, without the express written permission
of the author.

THIS BOOK IS DEDICATED TO MY
PARENTS.

Contents

Acknowledgements

First and foremost, I am grateful to God for making it possible for me to write this book. I would also like to express gratitude to the companies who gave me the opportunity to join their organizational learning and development teams. I owe to my managers for trusting me and to my colleagues for assisting me whenever needed. I am indebted to my hundreds of trainees who provided me with the feedback that helped me become better in facilitating customer service training. I appreciate all my customers who taught me the most about the art of customer service. Last, but not least, I thank my family for all their love and support.

Preface

This book is philosophical in the sense that it will make you rethink *Customer Service*, yet it is practical in value by giving you "real" tools that actually work—ones that are relevant to both small and large businesses. In addition, you will find hands-on activities in each chapter to apply what you have learned by putting things in *your* perspective. Thus, this book can be utilized in three ways:

a) To be utilized as a guide for *Customer Service* training meant to be delivered at seminars, institutes, and organizations.

b) To be utilized as a text for an introductory level business course with a focus on *Customer Service,* taught at a school, college, or university.

c) To be utilized as a "teach yourself" resource to learn the art of *Customer Service* and to discuss what you learn with your colleagues in meetings or focus groups.

The objectives of learning and development are as follows:

1. To share with you the *3C*—the driving force behind the multi-billion dollar *Customer Service* industry.

2. To make available to you a *formula* to calculate the actual worth of your customer in dollars and cents.

3. To redefine *Customer Service* announcing the *360* model.

4. To go inside the hidden mindsets of *8i* customers and coach you on how to approach them with confidence while responding to their needs and wants with "know how".

5. To give you the *power* to stay in full control even in some of the most difficult situations—unpleasant and uncertain—striking a fine balance between what is right for the customer and good for your business.

6. To show you how to *save* your customers without having to say *yes* to their demands.

7. To enlighten you with *four* ways to overcome communication barriers and connect with your customers in a manner that eradicates the roots of misinterpretation and lays solid grounds for understanding.

8. To provide you with *three* tips on finding "simple" solutions to "complex" problems.

9. To put in plain words the value of time by: setting the expectations, counting every minute, and offering additional assistance.

10. To discuss the three factors to keep in mind when educating customers: the *human* element, *Objection* vis-à-vis *Rejection*, who makes the *final call.*

11. To elaborate the impact of *3D*—Discuss, Define, Document—when it comes to *agreements* signed between you and your customers so that your customers don't get surprises and you don't get headaches if things don't go as expected.

12. To make you exceed your customer expectations by employing **3A**—Advise, Assure, Appreciate.

13. To let you establish long-term relationships with your customers that result in lasting loyalty and sustained profitability.

14. To clarify one common misconception about 7%-38%-55% Rule on how our *words*, *tone*, and *body language* impact how others perceive us and our message.

15. To put the three levels of communication—face-to-face, over-the-phone, online—in context so *you* decide what works best for you and your customers.

Activity 1 – *Customer Service* and you

Before we get started, please take a moment to write a few words on why *Customer Service* is important to you; what aspect of *Customer Service* you find challenging; and what you hope to gain from reading this book.

Why Customer Service?

Ever wonder why there is so much buzz about providing great *Customer Service* in today's business world? Why organizations small to large are spending gazillions in order to improve their *Customer Service,* which (unlike *Sales*) in and of itself does not make any money for them? And perhaps most importantly, why spend all this capital on

> "THE CUSTOMER EXPERIENCE IS THE NEXT COMPETITIVE BATTLEGROUND."
>
> -JERRY GREGOIRE

Customer Service instead of on promoting our products or services more and offering them to the customers at even more competitive prices? Well, it boils down to three factors—I call them *3C*:

1. Customer's self-respect

2. Competition

3. Cost of losing a customer

Let's talk about it …

What Customers value most

Plain and simple—themselves! Is there anyone who would disagree that Lexus is a high quality product? Probably not! Yet, I came across this lady from Nebraska who was looking for a new car for herself; walked out of a Lexus dealership and ended up buying an Acura. Not because she couldn't afford it and yes she did believe in Lexus. You may have guessed by now; she didn't think that she was treated right at the Lexus dealership. Guess what? She valued herself more than her favourite car

> "YOUR CUSTOMER DOESN'T CARE HOW MUCH YOU KNOW UNTIL THEY KNOW HOW MUCH YOU CARE."
>
> -DAMON RICHARDS

(Lexus). Perhaps she settled for something equally good (Acura) but that's not what was originally on her mind. By the way, we aren't comparing Lexus with Acura. Regardless of what she could have got for herself instead—Mercedes-Benz, Cadillac, Infiniti (you name it)—the fact remains that it's the *Customer Service* she experienced that changed her mind. On how many occasions have you considered taking your business elsewhere because you felt that you were not being valued as a customer? Why would anyone go back to a place and spend money where one is not respected?

Is there an exception? Yes, someone in a desperate situation will make an exception! Say, Mr. Customer's child is suffering from asthma and they ran out of the (life saving) drug. Say, the customer lives in the countryside and can get the drug from only two possible pharmacies—*Store A* and *Store B*—both located within a reasonable driving distance. *Customer Service* at *Store A* is very rude and unfriendly, yet the life saving drug they carry meets every required standard of quality, it's priced right, and the medicine is sitting on the shelf ready to be consumed immediately. On the other hand, *Store B* is where you'd find the friendliest pharmaceutical service you could receive; however, the same life saving medicine expired 24 hours ago (quality is at risk), or they are charging 3 times more than that of *Store A* (can't afford it), or it's going to take two days to get the medicine delivered (unavailability when needed). In this extreme situation, the customer is left with no choice but to go for *Store A* even though they don't treat their customers with reverence. That leads us into discussing the 2nd factor that we mentioned above that makes *Customer Service* so crucial for the success of a business—Competition.

Why Competition leads to better Customer Service

Today's intense competition and global economy provide more choices for customers than ever before. The hypothetical scenario discussed above is not what most of us go through in our daily lives. From life saving drugs to pure luxury items, from consumer goods such as cars to industrial products such as cranes, from tangible items such as high definition TV to intangible services such as satellite TV

> "BEING ON PAR IN TERMS OF PRICE AND QUALITY ONLY GETS YOU INTO THE GAME. SERVICE WINS THE GAME."
>
> -TONY ALLESANDRA

channels, customers may choose one vendor over the other. So companies better not focus only on the quality, price, and availability of their products and services, but also on their customers.

Today's competitive markets have almost eradicated any monopoly that once existed in many business sectors and given the power of choice back to the customers. Acceptable quality, competitive prices, and prompt delivery are now offered by many, not few. This is why the human element plays a key role in *Customer Service* and is often *the* deciding factor whether a customer is going to choose to stay with a business or leave for a competitor.

Say Ms. Smith who spends on average $50.00 a month on her cell phone bill doesn't receive courteous customer service from her wireless service provider so she decides to switch to a competitor. One may argue what is the big deal about $50/month revenue (cost of losing a customer) for a multi-billion dollar wireless industry. What's at stake is a lot more than $50.00 a month in revenue. This leads us to our 3rd and final factor that makes *Customer Service* one of the focal points for both small and large businesses—Cost of losing a Customer.

Why Cost of losing a Customer is a big deal

The truth of the matter is that offering excellent *Customer Service* is not the ultimate goal in and of itself for any business. In fact, it's simply a way to **gain lasting loyalty and aim for sustained profitability,** which is the only way an organization can stay in business. One must realize that gaining customer loyalty is a prerequisite to aiming for a sustained profitability. In other words, improving customer satisfaction with your business translates directly to your bottom line. How? Well, the numbers don't lie! Check this out...

> "IT'S ALL ABOUT NUMBERS, NUMBERS, NUMBERS."
>
> ·JOHN ILHAN

➢ It costs between five and six times more to attract a new customer than to keep an existing customer.

➢ Companies can boost profits from 25 percent to 125 percent by retaining 5 percent more existing customers.

➢ Only one out of 25 dissatisfied customers will express dissatisfaction to you.

➢ Happy customers tell at least four others of a positive experience. Dissatisfied customers tell as many as 12 about a negative experience.

➢ Two-thirds of customers do not feel valued by those serving them.

➢ A 2 percent increase in customer retention has the same effect on profits as cutting costs by 10 percent.

➢ The average company loses 10 percent of its customers each year.

➢ The customer profitability rate tends to increase over the life of a retained customer.

Source: Extreme Management, Mark Stevens, 2001; Leading on the Edge of Chaos, Emmett C. Murphy and Mark A. Murphy, 2003

Going back to Ms. Smith who decided to leave her *Good Old* wireless service provider, now that we have such alarming statistics, let's do some arithmetic.

Life Time Revenue (LTR)

Say Ms. Smith is 25 years old and has plans to keep her wireless service for the rest of her life. Assuming she is a potential cell phone user for the next 40 years to come. So the *life time revenue* (LTR) of Ms. Smith is going to be $24,000 ($50, the amount she spends per month on wireless bill * 40, the number of years she'd potentially remain a wireless customer * 12, number of months in a year). No, it doesn't stop here.

> "THERE IS ONLY ONE BOSS — THE CUSTOMER. AND HE CAN FIRE EVERYBODY IN THE COMPANY FROM THE CHAIRMAN ON DOWN, SIMPLY BY SPENDING HIS MONEY SOMEWHERE ELSE."
>
> -SAM WALTON

Attracting a new customer

We just learned from the above stats that it costs 5 to 6 times more to attract a new customer than to keep an existing one. This means that the *Good Old* wireless company will have to spend at least $300 ($50.00 * 6) in marketing to gain a new customer to replace the lost revenue no longer earned through Ms. Smith.

> "EVERY CLIENT YOU KEEP IS ONE LESS THAT YOU NEED TO FIND."
>
> -NIGEL SANDERS

Sharing frustration

What about the cost of sharing frustration? An unhappy customer shares his or her negative experience with as many as 12 others. Even if only 25% of the dozen people who come to know Ms. Smith's story decide to stay away from this company, there goes another $72,000 ($24,000 * 3) in lost potential revenue for the *Good Old* wireless service.

> "IF YOU MAKE CUSTOMERS UNHAPPY IN THE PHYSICAL WORLD, THEY MIGHT EACH TELL 6 FRIENDS. IF YOU MAKE CUSTOMERS UNHAPPY ON THE INTERNET, THEY CAN EACH TELL 6,000 FRIENDS."
>
> -JEFF BEZOS

Power of word-of-mouth

Let's not forget the cost that comes as a result of the missed opportunity for word-of-mouth advertisement. In other words, if Ms. Smith had been very happy with her service, she'd have shared her positive experience with at least four others within her circle of family and friends. Even if one out of four would have chosen

> "PROFIT IN BUSINESS COMES FROM REPEAT CUSTOMERS; CUSTOMERS THAT BOAST ABOUT YOUR PRODUCT AND SERVICE, AND THAT BRING FRIENDS WITH THEM."
>
> -EDWARDS DEMING

Good Old wireless on Ms. Smith's recommendation that would have brought $24,000—now lost potential business.

The bottom line

Add up all the numbers and you find that it can potentially cost *Good Old* wireless $120,300 in lost revenue over the next 40 years for not being able to save Ms. Smith's customer loyalty. Who would have thought that *life time revenue* of an average customer could end up in six figures? If one argues why care about that $50 a month, someone is not doing the math!

> "GOOD CUSTOMER SERVICE COSTS LESS THAN BAD CUSTOMER SERVICE"
>
> -SALLY GRONOW

Your reputation

We must remember that the potential lost revenue discussed above is as a result of *one* unhappy customer leaving the company. You can imagine if Ms. Smith is treated by *Good Old* wireless service in such a way that she decides to leave and take her business elsewhere, there is a good chance that other customers (could be hundreds or even thousands) will also leave this company, resulting in millions of dollars in lost business. But you know what? *Good Old* wireless service lost something that is even more valuable than the six figure revenue over the life time of this one customer, and that is its reputation among the customer's friends and family and perhaps even beyond. No matter what business you are in, you can't put a price tag on reputation; it's priceless!

> "IT TAKES 20 YEARS TO BUILD A REPUTATION AND FIVE MINUTES TO RUIN IT. IF YOU THINK ABOUT THAT, YOU'LL DO THINGS DIFFERENTLY."
>
> -WARREN BUFFETT

Activity 2 – Life time Value

Please take a moment to relate all this to your own line-of-business. Take an average customer of yours as an example and fill in the table provided below. Alternatively, think of a situation when you decided to take your business elsewhere, calculate the financial impact as a result of you leaving the company.

Item#	[i]Category	Calculation
a	[ii]Monthly revenue	
b	[iii]Customer's approximate age	
c	[iv]Potential number of years this customer will stay with the company (65 minus b)	
d	[v]Life time revenue of a customer (a * 12 * c)	
e	[vi]Cost to replace an existing customer	
f	[vii]Cost of sharing frustration (d * 3)	
g	[viii]Loss of potential business as a result of word-of-mouth advertisement that never occurred	
h	[ix]**Life time Value** **(d + e + f + g)**	

---

[i] The suggested numbers for each of the categories can differ based on the nature of business and demographics; please adjust any of the numbers, accordingly

[ii] The average revenue a typical customer brings to the organization on a monthly basis

[iii] Consider usual age group of your customer base and then take the average

[iv] Average life expectancy may differ based on geographical region and ethnicity

[v] Please note that it's the *revenue* that we're calculating and not the *net-profit*

[vi] Take your annual marketing budget and divide it by the approximate number of new customers joining per annum

[vii] Assume that customer speaks negatively to twelve individuals but only impacts the decision making of three of them i.e. 25%

[viii] Assume you get only one new customer from the customer's circle of family and friends; same result as item *d*

[ix] The life time value indicates the total potential revenue (again not the net-profit) the customer can bring during the

Activity 3 – Define *Customer Service*

In a group or individually, come up with your own definition of *Customer Service*.

Activity 4 – Can anyone describe an elephant?

Now, here comes a challenge as big as an elephant. How will you describe an elephant to someone who has never seen one? Can you put it in words?

You must be wondering what the connection is; read on …

Define *Customer Service* but wait, first describe what an elephant looks like

If you ask your colleagues to define *Customer Service*, you may get answers along these lines: *Customer Service* is all about treating customers with respect; *Customer Service* is focusing on customer needs; *Customer Service* is providing fast and friendly service. All of the answers are great but is there anything missing? Are we really looking at *Customer Service* from *360 degrees*?

Say you drop by your favourite coffee shop and ask for a decaffeinated coffee *with* cream but *no* sugar; while you get prompt and friendly service, you end up getting black coffee (*no* cream, *no* sugar). In other words, **the service is <u>efficient</u> but not <u>effective</u>.** Are you going to be a happy camper? On the other hand, what if you were welcomed with a big smile and a perfect cup of coffee exactly as you asked for it, but you had to wait for thirty minutes to get the cup of coffee? **The service is <u>effective</u> but not <u>efficient</u>.** Will you be satisfied? Looks like neither efficiency nor effectiveness alone can please a customer.

Defining *Customer Service* reminds me of the story of the elephant and the six blind men.

Once upon a time, there lived six blind men in a village. One day the villagers told them, "Hey, there is an elephant in the village today." They had no idea what an elephant was. They decided, "Even though we would not be able to see it, let us go and feel it anyway." All of them went where the elephant was. Every one of them touched the elephant.

"Hey, the elephant is a pillar," said the first man who touched his leg.

"No! It is like a rope," said the second man who touched the tail.

"Sorry but actually it is like a thick branch of a tree," said the third man who touched the trunk of the elephant.

"What are you guys talking about? It is like a big hand fan" said the fourth man who touched the ear of the elephant.

"Are you all trying to make a fool out of me? It is like a huge wall," said the fifth man who touched the belly of the elephant.

"Okay folks, enough! It is like a solid pipe," said the sixth man who touched the tusk of the elephant.

They began to argue about the elephant and every one of them insisted that he was right. It looked like they were getting agitated. A wise man was passing by and he saw this. He stopped and asked them, "What is the matter?" They said, "We cannot agree on what the elephant is like." Each one of them told what he thought the elephant was like. The wise man calmly explained to them, "All of you are right. The reason every one of you is telling it differently is because each one of you touched a different part of the elephant. So, actually the elephant has all those features that you all said."

"Oh!" everyone said.

Introducing *Customer Service 360*

Various answers typically happen when we try to define *Customer Service*. But what businesses need and customers demand is what I call, *Customer Service 360*, which looks at *Customer Service* from *all* sides i.e. 360 degrees. At times, the answer we're looking for is hidden in the very question we're asking. All we have to do is to just step back and take a look at our question itself. That's what I discovered as I pondered over finding a comprehensive and concise definition of *Customer Service*. I found the answer in my very question; all I had to do is simply flip the two words;

after all in order to provide …

"CUSTOMER SERVICE" (Noun)

don't we …

"SERVICE CUSTOMER" (Verb)?

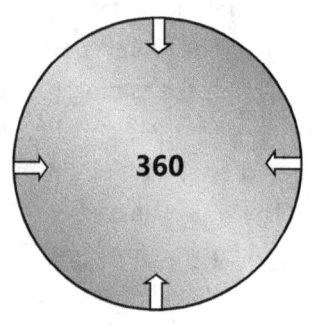

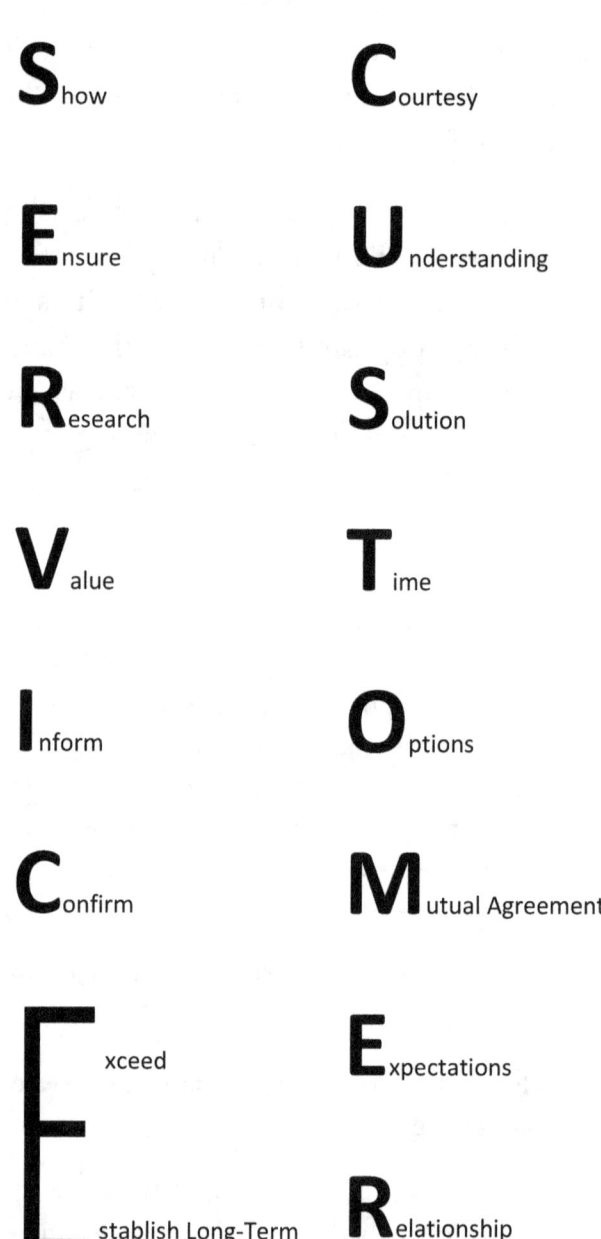

Show   **C**ourtesy

Ensure   **U**nderstanding

Research   **S**olution

Value   **T**ime

Inform   **O**ptions

Confirm   **M**utual Agreement

Exceed   **E**xpectations

Establish Long-Term   **R**elationship

Customer Service 360 Benefits Who?

Who can benefit from this model? The beauty of the model is that it is simple to understand and easy to apply, yet powerful enough to benefit the *Customer Service Professionals* who apply it, the *Customers* who experience it, and the *Companies* who choose to make it part of their strategic business action plan.

SHOW COURTESY

ENSURE UNDERSTANDING

RESEARCH SOLUTION

VALUE TIME

INFORM OPTIONS

CONFIRM MUTUAL AGREEMENT

EXCEED EXPECTATIONS

ESTABLISH LONG-TERM RELATIONSHIP

Benefiting *Customer Service Professionals*

This model benefits the *Customer Service Professionals* by providing them with the tools they need to take care of their customers, even in some of the most difficult and challenging situations. It helps them better understand the eight types of customers (discussed later) who they interact with on a daily basis. Not only that, the model enhances one's communication skills in terms of what to say, when to say it, and how to say it, in order to build a sound rapport with the customer. The model also provides a logical approach to understanding a customer's underlying concerns and issues and provides strategies to offer solutions that meet the needs of customers in a timely manner. As a result, *Customer Service Professionals* enjoy the confidence, job satisfaction, and high self-esteem that can only come when you've a sense that what you do is making a difference and that you're good at what you do!

> "ONLY A LIFE LIVED IN THE SERVICE TO OTHERS IS WORTH LIVING."
>
> -ALBERT EINSTEIN

Benefiting *Customers*

This model (when applied) benefits the customers because they are treated with high regard. Those assisting them actively listen to their concerns and act upon it effectively and efficiently—*doing right things* and *doing things right*. The solutions offered to customers are tailored to their individual needs—no more cookie cutter approach. Customers are educated and provided with options, enabling

> "IT STARTS WITH RESPECT. IF YOU RESPECT THE CUSTOMER AS A HUMAN BEING, AND TRULY HONOR THEIR RIGHT TO BE TREATED FAIRLY AND HONESTLY, EVERYTHING ELSE IS MUCH EASIER."
>
> -DOUG SMITH

them to make informed decisions so they are getting the best value for their money. The vendors are not only meeting but exceeding their expectations; which will in turn give customers a true sense of satisfaction from being valued and treated with a sense of urgency and priority!

Benefiting *Companies*

Companies get enormous benefit from the model by having their employees, *Customer Service Professionals* take pride in their job, which results in lower turnover cost and higher productivity. The companies will also enjoy a customer base who loves to stay loyal providing sustained profitability as well as on-going growth. How come growth? Well, happy customers tend to launch the most effective, yet free-of-cost, marketing campaigns for the companies known as "word-of-mouth", which brings more business and greater profits. Such additional profits enable companies to

> "IF YOU DO BUILD A GREAT EXPERIENCE, CUSTOMERS TELL EACH OTHER ABOUT THAT. WORD OF MOUTH IS VERY POWERFUL."
>
> -JEFF BEZOS

offer better products to the customers giving them even better value for their money. With soaring profits, companies can also offer superior incentives to their employees. When employees feel they are appreciated, they'll also tend to stay faithful to their companies, which in turn reduce the high cost of hiring and training new recruits, which results in even higher profits for the companies.

In short, *CUSTOMER SERVICE 360* creates a true *win-win-win* situation for the *Customer Service Professionals*, the *Customers*, and the *Companies*. So let's dive in.

I - SHOW COURTESY

We all know that we need to show courtesy to every customer but isn't courtesy subjective as opposed to objective? What may sound courteous to one, could be perceived otherwise by another; reason being, we also have to deal with customers at an emotional level that makes providing courteous customer service challenging, to say the least. Likewise, to ensure that you truly understand a customer's concern is oftentimes not black and white especially when the customer isn't expressive enough.

The first and foremost element of excellent customer service is to show courtesy every time we interact with a customer—every business owes this to its customers. Well, there is good news and bad news. The bad news is that the business community loses customers every single day because their customer service lacks the element of courtesy. The good news is that showing courtesy is as easy as 1-2-3 if you follow the *Do's* and *Don'ts*.

3 Don'ts – (a) Don't Ignore (b) Don't Argue (c) Don't Lie ... Ever!

There is really not much to add, but I'll say this ... if we want our customers to believe that we value their business then we better not ignore their issues; if we respect their opinion regarding their experiences with our products and services then we better not argue with them when they bring their concerns to us; and last but not the least, if we want our customer to trust us then we better never lie to them—it is not only a better business practice but also (ethically and morally) the right thing to do.

> "IN OUR WAY OF WORKING, WE ATTACH A GREAT DEAL OF IMPORTANCE TO HUMILITY AND HONESTY; WITH RESPECT FOR HUMAN VALUES, WE PROMISE TO SERVE OUR CUSTOMERS WITH INTEGRITY."
>
> ·AZIM PREMJI

3 Do's (a) Smile Sincerely (b) Approach Appropriately (c) Respond Reasonably ... Always!

(a) Smile Sincerely

Let's welcome each customer with a sincere smile. One may ask, smiling in a face-to-face interaction makes sense, but what about when dealing with a customer over the phone or providing online assistance over the Internet through chat? I'll come back to this question later. Let me first address why smile? You probably have heard the old proverb, "*An apple a day keeps the doctor away*". I say, "*Many smiles a day help keep our customers from going away*".

> "A MAN WITHOUT A SMILING FACE MUST NOT OPEN A SHOP."
>
> -CHINESE PROVERB

Smiling not only brings joy to one's facial expression, but can also make the brain produce endorphins which reduce physical and emotional pain, and give a greater sense of well-being. How can you possibly take care of your customers unless you're relaxed yourself and your customer is comfortable with you? A sincere smile can do the magic!

Once, I along with my colleagues was on a business trip to Franklin, Tennessee where we were served at a local restaurant by a server with a cold attitude; later we all left leaving no tips. Also, although we did consider going to back to the same restaurant the next day, as it was just across the road from our hotel at a walking distance and the food was indeed good, we didn't. We took the car and the trouble to drive around and find a different restaurant. It doesn't cost a penny to smile at someone, yet it makes a whole world of difference as to how others perceive you and the business you represent. With that said, make sure the smile is sincere; a fake one will do no good to anyone.

Going back to smiling over the phone; it may sound silly but customers can hear our smiles. Obviously, I don't mean literally, but for sure, figuratively. Smile; a facial expression will actually change the tone of our voice in a positive way i.e. making our voice sound more pleasant and welcoming. As for online customer service, I wouldn't suggest putting an emoticon for a smiley face ☺ in your email correspondence to a customer who is complaining about some on-going issue, but if we know the customer very well and have developed that kind of rapport and know for sure what the limits are in terms of staying professional with that customer, then using a smiley in one's email or during online live customer support can actually lighten both parties and help create a friendly atmosphere in which the customer can be served best. I'd check the company policy or ask the management before changing the face of my email or chat session. If you are in doubt, I suggest that you stay away from all emoticons and be safe rather than sorry.

Our smile is part of non-verbal communication. You may have come across the 7%-38%-55% Rule which attempts to put weight on the relative significance of words, tone of voice, and body posture; at times this rule is misinterpreted. I have dealt with the subject separately in Appendix One.

(b) Approach Appropriately

Let's approach appropriately when encountering a customer using a simple three-step process—Greeting Customer, Introducing Yourself, and Offering Assistance.

1) Greeting Customer

One should always approach a customer with a greeting appropriate to one's business culture and to the customer's expectations, such as *"Good Morning, Good Afternoon, or Good Evening"*. Or it can be a little bit less formal, such as *"Hello and Hi"*. In no way is a formal or an informal greeting better than the other as long as it is consistent with the company policy, acceptable within the business culture, and last but not the least, okay with your customer. The idea is to make the customer feel welcomed (this time verbally; remember we've already made the customer feel comfortable non-verbally with the smile). In today's global economy, your customer may belong to a different culture or speak a different language. You may choose to greet your customers coming from diversified backgrounds

> "MAKE IT EASY FOR YOUR CUSTOMERS TO TALK TO YOU."
>
> -KEVIN STIRTZ

using their own language; by taking this extra step, you make them feel even more at ease. You can easily look up any key phrase such as how to say hello in world languages using your favourite search engine to be able to greet your diversified customer base in their first language. You may also run into customers who use sign language; the word hello is signed by moving the hand away from the forehead in a forward and downward motion, similar to a salute.

2) Introducing Yourself

Once the customer starts to feel welcome as we greet him or her, the next step is to introduce ourselves by providing our name and perhaps even our job title and the department we work for, so the customer knows if he or she is speaking to the right person. If assisting over the phone, do mention your company's name as well. One may ask, isn't that common sense? That's true but unfortunately there are folks out there representing their respective businesses without necessarily introducing themselves, thereby creating this communication gap between them and their potential or existing customers. For example, once I called this courier service to mail a package, a person picked up the phone, said, *"Yes"* and then there was a dead silence (no introduction and no offer to assist). If you have been in a similar situation, you can imagine how awkward it feels. The idea of introducing yourself is to let the customer feel that you are personally taking *ownership* of the customer's needs. By the way, it also helps to have the customer introduce himself or herself (to get his or her name), then try to use the customer's name during the conversation. Calling someone by his or her name is really the first step one may take to personalize the interaction—no matter how successful or large a business is, we need to treat our customers as *individuals* not as *numbers*. You may do so by simply asking, *"May I know your name please"*. If the name is too difficult to pronounce or unfamiliar, it doesn't hurt to ask the customer for the correct pronunciation or even ask them to spell it for you. Using Sir or Ma'am is considered acceptable across many business cultures but addressing someone by his or her name should always be preferred. Whether you should address customers with their first name or last name depends on what is most acceptable to the individual customer and your company policy. The key is to strike a balance between what is professional and what is friendly. Using one's last

> "IT HELPS A TON WHEN YOU LEARN PEOPLE'S NAMES AND DON'T BUTCHER THEM WHEN TRYING TO PRONOUNCE THEM."
>
> -JERRY YANG

name is generally considered more professional whereas using the first name is friendlier. If not sure, simply get the customer's permission to call him or her by their first name. I'd suggest checking your company policy on the subject, if any. If there isn't one out there, then use your common sense and what you deem acceptable and appropriate.

3) Offering Assistance

The next step is offering assistance such as, *"How can I help you?"* or *"How may I assist you?"* The idea behind offering assistance is to find out exactly what it is that the customer is looking for and not to jump into any assumptions even if we've served the same customer in the past. A colleague of mine once went to a mall to buy a suit and the only reason he chose to walk out of the store without buying anything is because the sales person who wasn't even busy with any other customer, still didn't bother to come up to him and offer assistance.

> "MORE BUSINESS IS LOST EVERY YEAR THROUGH NEGLECT THAN THROUGH ANY OTHER CAUSE."
>
> -ROSE KENNEDY

Approaching Appropriately by using this simple three-step process (introducing, greeting, and offering assistance) is time and again proven to build a quick rapport with a customer. This approach has been practised by successful businesses over centuries and there is no need to change it, as per the popular words of wisdom, *"Don't fix if it isn't broke"*.

Activity 5 – Greet and introduce

Please take a moment to write your own standard business greeting—one that is appropriate to your business culture and acceptable to your customers. Also, note down the way you introduce yourself and the department/line-of-business your represent. Finally, put pen to paper, how will you have your customer introduce him or herself?

Given your situation, put a check next to the option that best works for you, your customer, and your business:

☐ Mostly, I call my customers by their *last* name.

☐ Mostly, I call my customers by their *first* name.

Discussion Point (optional): If you're receiving this customer service training in a group environment, talk about it with your colleagues or other trainees; what difference it makes if any, whether you call a customer by their first or last name.

c) Respond Reasonably

Many years in the customer service industry have taught me that basically a customer can come up to us with any of *eight* mind sets—let's refer to them as *8i*. If it is vital to respond reasonably to each and every customer then it is imperative to understand the customer's mindset. Here they are...

1) INTERESTED   *5) I DON'T MIND*

2) I COMPARE   *6) IMPATIENT*

3) I KNOW   *7) IRATE*

4) INDECISIVE   *8) IT'S OVER*

The question is, how do we get to know which *8i* we are facing? And how do we deal with each of those unique situations during our interaction with the customer? This is how it's done...

INTERESTED customers

Customer's Mindset:
I would like to know *more* about what you have to offer me.

How to find out if you're dealing with **INTERESTED** *customers:*
These customers are likely to make some reference to an advertisement they saw on TV; a promotion they came across on the web; or simply a word-of-mouth reference they got from a friend. By the way, they may not mention any of the above; rather simply show interest in your products or services. For example, if this customer wants to buy a car, you might hear from the customer, *"Looks like you've some great deals going on your New Year models; tell me about it"*.

Reasonable Response to **INTERESTED** *customers:*
It's a matter of courtesy that our natural response should be to find out what it is that made the customer interested in our products or services and to try to find out their needs and wants. You may want to find out how they learned about your products or services. Once

> "EVERY CONTACT WE HAVE WITH A CUSTOMER INFLUENCES WHETHER OR NOT THEY'LL COME BACK. WE HAVE TO BE GREAT EVERY TIME OR WE'LL LOSE THEM."
>
> ·KEVIN STIRTZ

you understand where the customer is coming from, you can educate the customer on your products; highlighting the key **features** and most importantly translating those features into **benefits**. To put this into perspective, say a college student is interested in leasing a car.

Having an idea of the customer's needs, it would only make sense to start with compact cars with low monthly payments, while mentioning the gas mileage one gets out of the car (a feature), and how much money one may save on gas (a benefit).

I COMPARE customers

Customer's Mindset:
I am willing to give you my business only if you can offer me something *better* than your competitor.

How to find out if you're dealing with **I COMPARE** *customers:*
They are likely going to mention your competition somewhere in conversation. If this customer wants to buy a car, he'll probably say, *"The dealer across the street is offering 0% financing on the latest models for 24 months with $2000 down, can you beat that?"* At times you may not hear a word about your competitor; instead, you'll be reminded of what kind of deal you offered to another customer and now your potential *I COMPARE* customer needs something similar. For lack of a better term we'll call it the *"me-too"* situation, where a customer compares himself or herself with his or her friend and expects to get a similar deal.

Reasonable Response to **I COMPARE** *customers:*
For those who want to beat their competition, focus on the ***advantages*** your product has over that of your competitors with honesty. Knowledge of what your competition offers (besides your own product line) is essential to effectively dealing with *I COMPARE* customers, which wasn't the case in taking care of *INTERESTED* customers.

In case of a *"me-too"* situation see if you can offer this customer exactly what was offered to his or her friend, knowing this is not always possible. Perhaps the friend was a long time customer with potential life time revenue much higher than that of an average customer, making him or her more deserving of the kind of deal that he or she got. Maybe there was a sale going on at the time that got him or her a deal and now the sale is over. What if the friend was offered extra compensation for something that went wrong with your product or service, so your company went above and beyond not to lose his or her customer loyalty. There may now be external reasons such as a change in the economy or market conditions preventing you from offering similar deals to any new customer. The point is there could be numerous factors as to why a deal once available can't be offered anymore. Regardless of the situation, you should first politely explain to the customer why you're *not* in a position to offer exactly what was offered before, but then immediately get to the promotions that are currently available and that will make this potential customer feel that he or she is still getting a deal (even though not exactly

> "IF WE DON'T TAKE CARE OF OUR CUSTOMERS, SOMEONE ELSE WILL."
>
> -UNKNOWN

the same he or she had expected). Bottom line is that you want to make this potential customer believe that you are going the *extra mile* and that he or she is valued just like his or her friend. If no deals are presently available, but something is coming up shortly then let the customer know and set proper expectations such as providing him with a specific date as to when to check back with you later. Even better, instead of asking the customer to contact you, see if you can commit yourself to getting in touch with the customer at the time of promotion, lest the customer forgets about you and takes his or her business elsewhere. In those situation where you just don't have any deals going on now or are expecting one anytime soon, see if you can use your empowerment (your decision making authority) or your manager's approval to offer him or her something better than simply sticking to the regular price, even if it means adding some goodies (extra stuff). If that's not even an option, simply apologize, explain your position and offer whatever you can to get the customer the best possible choices currently available.

I KNOW customers

Customer's Mindset:
I know what I want so please keep your recommendations to yourself and give me *exactly* what I am asking for.

How to find out if you're dealing with **I KNOW** *customers:*
They'll sound confident, straightforward, and to the point; in addition, they will be very specific as to what they want. Someone with this mindset who is interested in buying a car would express something like, *"I am looking for a 6-cylinder 4-door sedan with automatic transmission, air-conditioning, and cruise control having absolutely no more than 36,000 clicks on it."*

Reasonable Response to **I KNOW** *customers:*
Believe it or not, these customers are perhaps the easiest to handle since they let you know exactly what it would take to get their business—you don't even have to probe them! Simply offer these customers exactly what they're looking for and you're done. However, if what is being asked is not available then propose something close enough. But remember to let them know *precisely* where your product falls short of their demands. The only time I'll give my personal opinion to such a customer is when I

> "IF YOU HELP ENOUGH PEOPLE GET WHAT THEY WANT, YOU WILL GET WHAT YOU WANT."
>
> -ZIG ZIGLAR

realize that the customer is missing out on some critical factors regarding product knowledge; however, my opinion will be in a tone of passing information and not in the form of making a suggestion. Bottom line, pay close attention to the details you gather from such customers and then respond in definite terms and avoid dwelling in generalities—keep it concise and straightforward—you'll find these customers will take no time in making a decision and also be satisfied with it; making your job a whole lot easier.

INDECISIVE customers

Customer's Mindset:
I'm *not sure* what I want; I need someone to help me out.

How to find out if you're dealing with **INDECISIVE** *customers:*
These customers are exactly the opposite of *I KNOW* customers. You'll spot them by finding that they speak to you in vague and general terms with no specifics; in addition, they'll easily switch their interest from one product to another. Such a customer interested in buying a car will probably say, *"I am looking for a relatively new car ... but I don't want to pay too much for it ... do you have any SUVs or minivans ... hmm ... I don't know ... I wonder if I should just get a compact size car to save myself on gas".*

Reasonable Response to **INDECISIVE** *customers:*
You should start by probing using a combination of both closed-ended and open-ended questions with limited options for the customer to choose from, to find out exactly what would meet their needs best and then offer them what you've got, accordingly. When asking an open-ended question, such as *"May I ask what price range you are looking at?"* If possible, it should be followed by some limited choices, such as *"say under $5000, $5000-$7,000, $8,000-10,000."* Closed-ended questions that can only be answered in a *yes* or a *no* greatly help zoom into customer needs. For example, *"Does the colour of the vehicle really matter to you?"* One caution though in dealing with *INDECISIVE* customers, even though they rely on you to

> "THE MORE YOU ENGAGE WITH CUSTOMERS THE CLEARER THINGS BECOME AND THE EASIER IT IS TO DETERMINE WHAT YOU SHOULD BE DOING."
>
> -JOHN RUSSELL

choose what they want, never ever make a decision for them or single out one option for them or else be prepared to take the blame and be held responsible if things don't go as expected. Instead, based on the customer's needs found through probing, provide limited choices highlighting the features, benefits and limitations of each of the options and then let the customer do the final pick. Remember your job is to help the customer make an informed decision; not to make one for them.

I DON'T MIND customers

Customer's Mindset:
I do have a problem but I don't mind as long as you *fix it.*

How to find out if you're dealing with **I DON'T MIND** *customers:*

Although they'll clearly mention what their issue is, they'll remain calm while giving you an opportunity to resolve it. Say this customer is having engine issues with a recently purchased vehicle; he will express more or less like this, *"I just bought this car last month; I see the engine light came on today. Could you please look into that for me?"*

Reasonable Response to **I DON'T MIND** *customers:*

This customer overall has been satisfied doing business with you until something went wrong. However, he or she is willing to work with you as long as the issue is being taken care of. Please don't take this customer for granted only because he or she is not screaming at you. Rather, take the golden opportunity to earn back the customer's trust and confidence by apologizing for the inconvenience and by promising a prompt resolution. For example, *"Mr. Smith, I am sorry for the trouble you've had to go through, I assure you that we'll do everything possible to get your car up and running. Let our mechanic look into the issue and we'll advise you of the time and cost involved in fixing the car. If this is something covered under warranty then you won't have to pay for either the parts or labor"*. Make sure to keep to your word and also keep the customer in the loop i.e. let him or her know right away if there is any change in the original estimate both in terms of time it may take to get it fixed or in terms of the cost of fixing it. Using this simple common-sense approach will turn *I DON'T MIND* customers back to satisfied customers.

> "CUSTOMERS DON'T EXPECT YOU TO BE PERFECT. THEY DO EXPECT YOU TO FIX THINGS WHEN THEY GO WRONG."
>
> -DONALD PORTER

IMPATIENT customers

Customer's Mindset:

I've got a problem but don't have time for an excuse; I need a *fix now.*

How to find out if you're dealing with **IMPATIENT** *customers:*

Rest assured, this customer will let you know that he or she is really short on time and quite likely you'll be given a time frame to get the matter resolved or else. You'll feel that you're being pushed in terms of time; before you can even start looking into a solution to the problem, you may be asked several times how long it will take before you're done. This customer with a car problem will probably say, *"I need my car fixed no later than 3 p.m. sharp; I've a family trip planned for this evening. Can you have it fixed in an hour?"*

Reasonable Response to **IMPATIENT** *customers:*

Since such a customer demands a true sense of urgency from you, let him or her know that you'll do everything possible to provide prompt and timely service. For example, *"Mr. Smith, I am sorry for the inconvenience but I assure that I'll have my mechanic look at your vehicle as a high priority."* It's best (if possible) to pull all the available resources to get the job done in a timely fashion as long as it doesn't jeopardize any prior commitments with other customers. Realistically, you may not always have the flexibility to bump this customer in the priority sequence or perhaps the job itself needs more time than what the customer is willing to spare; such time constraints can be best handled by looking at alternate solutions. For example in the case of a car problem, one may consider arranging a rental vehicle for the customer; the idea is to buy more time with less impact on the customer's life. Even if the job takes longer than expected, keep the customer informed so there are no more surprises. Once the customer starts to get the feeling that they are valued and the issue of time constraint is taken seriously and with priority, the customer will likely be willing to show more flexibility and allow extra time. Once you have the time on your side, it's just a matter to get things delivered and leave the customer satisfied.

> "IT IS IN THIS MOMENT YOU HAVE THE POWER TO BE THE SOLUTION!"
>
> -ILEANA KANE

IRATE customers

Customer's Mindset:
I am totally *frustrated*; now you better take care of this issue you caused or else...

*How to find out if you're dealing with **IRATE** customers:*
This is likely an existing customer who is enraged with what he or she is going through because the product or service failed to meet his or her expectations. They'll appear furious, angry, and at times just plain bitter. They may even be offensive using abusive language toward your product or company, and even to you, getting personal. Some of them may even go the extreme and threaten to sue the company and take it to court. Unlike the *I DON'T MIND* type, an *IRATE* customer who is going through the car trouble will express his contempt somewhat like this, *"You guys made me buy this piece of junk last month by lying to me saying it would run forever, it didn't even last 30 days before I had to bring this car back to you so you can bill me hundreds more ... what a rip off!"*

*Reasonable Response to **IRATE** customers:*
Have some *empathy* (not *sympathy*) toward this customer and try to understand where he or she is coming from by putting yourself in his or her shoes. True, no one likes to be yelled at especially when it's not your (personal) fault. Realize that this customer is not really upset at you. He or she is simply annoyed due to the inconvenience and has no patience to deal with it, or

> "YOUR MOST UNHAPPY CUSTOMERS ARE YOUR GREATEST SOURCE OF LEARNING."
>
> -BILL GATES

perhaps was just having a bad day and now this car problem on top of the other issues going on in life caused him or her to lose temper. Just imagine how you'd feel if you were to go through the same situation. Now, you may not choose to react like a typical *IRATE* customer, but to expect everyone has the same patience as you is not realistic either. My number one advice on how to respond to *IRATE* customers is not to take their tone, demeanour, and words personally, rather treat them with the understanding that he or she has nothing against you. Allow them to vent so they bring it out whatever they have to say— please don't interrupt and certainly don't ague (remember the 3 Don'ts). Fire needs fuel to burn, if it doesn't get it, it will die; more likely than not this is going to diffuse their anger. Not only that, letting customers vent while you listen gives you an opportunity to pick up the bits and pieces of information to find out the underlying cause of their frustration. Once this customer has nothing more to say, he or she will be more inclined to listen to you and to what you are going to do to get the matter resolved. Once they allow you to speak, your response will be similar to what you'll say to the *I DON'T MIND* customer. That is, offer an apology and give assurance that the issue will be dealt with promptly. For example, *"Mr. Smith, if I were you, I'd be upset too. Please accept my apology for all the inconvenience you have had to go through. Please give us an opportunity to fix the issue."* Unlike *I DON'T MIND* customer, *IRATE* customers at times don't mention the actual problem. This is what you need to find out; what happened that provoked the anger. You may want to follow up by saying, *"Mr. Smith, just so I understand.............."* (Paraphrase what you've learned so far about the issue at hand and probe if the underlying issue is still not clear).

The above-mentioned customer service skills are tested in real situations and they do work! I once dealt with a cell phone customer who was outraged because her bill was much higher than what she expected. She started the call wanting to sue the company. Alternatively, the call ended in her signing another year of contract with the company, happy and satisfied. She even complimented me saying *"You should get a raise for calming me down"*. Guess what, all I did is used the strategy described above. Initially, I simply allowed her to vent while paying close attention to her words to find the root cause of the issue. By the time she was done, I knew that the issue was her most recent bill with unexpected charges. Even though she was billed accurately, I still apologized for any misunderstanding and walked her though the bill explaining all the charges. I then offered a new promotion available through the company that would not only adjust her current bill which she was concerned about but that would also result in on-going savings for the next 12 months to come with signing a new one-year contract. Not taking things personally, treating the customer with respect and empathy, and negotiating with integrity put me in full control of regaining the customer's loyalty.

There are times when *IRATE* customers choose to use inappropriate language and may even get personally abusive. Most organizations usually have policies on to how to handle these situations such as advising the customer to refrain from using abusive words and after multiple unsuccessful attempts say three or so, letting a manager or supervisor handle the customer from that point on. When providing customer service over the phone, you may be allowed to disconnect the call after multiple reminders to the customer. When providing online customer service, you may be allowed to close the chat session if the customer is persistently making inappropriate remarks. If a customer threatens to destroy property or physically harm someone, you must bring this to the attention of those in charge immediately so that a decision can be made whether to involve a local law enforcement authority or not. Again, it's critical to know your organization's policy in place; if not sure, make sure to check with your management or the human resources department. I believe that being in customer service you are there to help and not to take personal abuse or threats. In my many years of working in the customer service industry, I can confidently say that such extreme situations rarely arise (if ever). In most cases, you can effectively control the situation by using the customer service approach discussed above turning *IRATE* customers into happy campers.

IT'S OVER customers

Customer's Mindset:
I am *done* with you.

How to find out if you're dealing with **IT'S OVER** *customers:*
These customers will indicate discontinuing your service or returning your product with the intention to never come back; at times without even giving you a reason. For example, this same car trouble customer may say, while it's in the garage being worked on or looked at, *"That's enough. I just can't put up with this anymore. I need my car keys back".*

Reasonable Response to **IT'S OVER** *customers:*
You're dealing with someone who is absolutely disappointed and who has lost any trust that you can deliver the goods or services to his or her satisfaction. This is really your **last chance** to save this customer. At minimum, you can offer an apology and a "reasonable" compensation for the inconvenience that customer had to go through; not only because this is the "right" thing to do but also because this will bring you hope to earn the customer back or at least save your reputation. But what if this is not sufficient to change the customer's mind?

> "DO RIGHT. DO YOUR BEST. TREAT OTHERS AS YOU WANT TO BE TREATED."
>
> -LOU HOLTZ

Perhaps, going above and beyond a "reasonable" reparation is needed to ensure the customer will not leave. The question is how to find out exactly what it would take to earn back the customer when the customer is not even willing to speak to us. Given the situation, guessing is certainly not a good idea; however, if you are experienced in dealing with similar situations in the past and know what works and what doesn't then use your discretion. What if you're not sure what can be done? Do you just let the customer walk away like that? If nothing seems to work and you have no idea how to proceed, just put the ball back in the customer's court; be polite but straightforward and directly ask the customer what it would take to save him or her as a customer. This is something I call *"Last Attempt to Save"*. For example, *"Mr. Smith, we truly value you as our customer and we certainly don't want to lose you, is there anything we can do to keep you as our valued customer"*. Depending on how the customer responds, you'll likely face one of two scenarios:

Scenario A: Customer asks you for a "fair and reasonable" compensation for the service or product that the customer paid for but that you didn't deliver as promised. In this situation, it only make sense – both ethically as well as a good business practice—to do exactly what is being asked for, not only to secure the customer's loyalty but also to save your integrity. If you are not in the position to make such a decision, talk to someone in your organization who can. Some organizations specifically maintain a *Retention Team* to keep the churn (customer base turnover) down. Remember, you'll probably never get this opportunity again and do whatever you can to get the matter back in control.

Scenario B: Customer asks you not only for a refund (as a result of service failure) but is also looking for a freebie because of the inconvenience he or she had to go through. If that's the case, you should still pay back the customer—the money customer spent but faced a product or service failure—even if it is not enough to *save* the customer, it may be sufficient to *save* your reputation. Is it not the "right" thing to do anyway? As for giving away the freebies, this is the time to think about the *Life time Value* (discussed earlier) of this customer and do some math to see how much you're going to lose if you let him or her just walk away. Say the customer is expected to bring about $5000 of profit in the next five years; don't you think that giving away $50 of free service to win back the customer is worth it? However, giving away $5000 is probably not a sound business decision since it will make this customer a "zero-profit" customer for the next five years. Can your business afford it? What if the customer decides to switch to your competitor anyway; that will result in a pure loss for your business. Striking a balance in what's good for the customer and for your business is the key!

By the way, something to consider while negotiating with a customer: not everyone demands that you go out of the way to save him. At times, all a customer wants is an **acknowledgement** and an **apology** (must be genuine) for the "service failure" that caused the customer some grief. Who really can't afford to give that to a customer?

Activity 6 – Share your challenge

Discuss within a group the last time you had to deal with a "difficult" customer. What was the *situation*? What *caused* it? How did you *deal* with it? How did it *turn out* at the end? Is there anything you would have done *differently* to handle the situation and *why*?

Facilitator's Tip: Split the learners into four groups and assign two of the *8i* to each of the groups.

Last word on Show Courtesy

This concludes the discussion not only on *8i* but also on the lesson, *Show Courtesy*. Before we move on to the next topic, I'd like to add that we cannot necessarily assume that the mindset of every single customer will exclusively fit the profile of only one of the *8i*. It's plausible for a customer to be *INTERESTED* in your new products and services but at the same time to have the mindset of being *I COMPARE* making sure to get the best deal in town. Also, a customer may switch from one mindset to another; for example, a customer may show up as an *I DON'T MIND* but when he or she notices that no one really cares about his or her problem, turns into an *"Irate"* customer. Upon continually being ignored (again, let's not forget the 3 Don'ts) may decide to be *IT'S OVER*. Regardless of what is on a customer's mind to begin with, our goal is to end every interaction with a sense that the customer is valued and was well taken care of. Metaphorically speaking, a customer is like a coin with two sides, where one side reflects **feelings & emotions** and the other side reflects **needs & wants**. The customer demands that we take care of him or her from both sides. If we show courtesy by smiling sincerely, approaching appropriately, and responding reasonably on each interaction, rest assured, we've dealt effectively with the customer's feelings and emotions (one side) and are well on our way to taking care of the other side of the coin by truly understanding their needs and wants (the other side).

II - ENSURE UNDERSTANDING

The second element of the *CUSTOMER SERVICE 360* model suggests flipping the coin and ensuring that we accurately understand every customer's needs and wants. To do so, we need to effectively utilize our **active listening and communication** skills. This step is so critical that if we fail here, at best, all subsequent efforts will go down the drain, leaving an unhappy customer; and at worst, we'll find the customer out the door, likely never to return back. What makes up communication? There are four pieces to this puzzle and they are...

1. *Originator* ... source that sends the message ...	e.g. Customer
2. *Message* ... point that is communicated from one to another ...	e.g. "I did not receive my last month's bill"
3. *Medium* ... means through which the message travels ...	e.g. Internet (Chat)
4. *Recipient* ... destination that receives the message ...	e.g. Customer Service Professional

During any customer interaction, we don't have much control over how clearly the *Originator* (read: *customer*) communicates the *Message* (read: *needs* & *wants*). When it comes to the *Medium*, there are three possibilities: we can be communicating with a customer face-to-face where the medium is *air*; via email or chat where the medium is *electronics*; or over the phone where the medium is a blend of both *air* and *electronics*. Discussing the three types of communication and evaluating which one will be preferred over another is a topic by itself so I have dealt with this subject separately in Appendix Two. Regardless of the type of medium being used, you can take practical steps to minimize the distractions that may jeopardize the communication process.

Rule # 1 – Remove all distractions

All distractions fall under two broad categories: External and Internal. External distractions (background noise, phone calls, etc.) are relatively easier to remove; for example, lowering music volume (if too loud); putting your cell phone on vibrate; are simple steps that will help you to stay focused when interacting with a customer. As you can imagine, things can only get worse if a customer has to repeat him or herself unnecessarily. As for the internal distractions (stress, inability to focus, etc.), though they're not as easy to handle, they can be managed as well.

> "WORK IS HARD. DISTRACTIONS ARE PLENTIFUL. AND TIME IS SHORT."
>
> -ADAM HOCHSCHILD

Healthy balanced food, regular exercise, good night sleep, effective time and money management, and better organizational skills will all help eliminate much of the stress. Simply taking a notepad and writing down all the things to do that are on our mind can clear the clutter and confusion that prevent us from focusing. Also, handling one customer at a time—both in person and in our thoughts—can help us minimize internal distractions. Say you had to deal with an *IRATE* customer a moment ago which put you in distress but now you have your next customer who's *INTERESTED*. It's neither fair to this customer nor to yourself to keep your mind engaged in what was said and what you could have done differently in dealing with the *IRATE* customer, or else there is a chance this *INTERESTED* customer will also turn into *IRATE*. If you can't stop thinking about the last customer, at times, even giving yourself a short break from work by stepping outside the building to catch some fresh air, taking a few deep breaths, or drinking a glass of water can all help take away the negativity and regain your ability to focus on your next customer.

Rule # 2 – Do not assume

Once we've achieved undivided attention toward the customer, it's very important to understand the message being communicated from the customer's perspective, not ours. Our perceptions usually come from our beliefs and past experiences that may carry us away from objectivity and lead us into baseless assumptions. When communicating with a customer, we tend to relate with similar situations we may have dealt with in the past. By the way, there is nothing wrong in doing so as long as it doesn't prevent us from finding all the facts *before* drawing any conclusions about the issue at hand. Although we may have handled similar types of customers before, the one you encounter next may have unique circumstances. Even if we've dealt with the same person, this time he or she may now have different priorities in life. Any interruption or filling in sentences for the customer can impair our ability to effectively understand the customer. Rather, we should be actively listening to what the customer has to say and take mental notes of the key points. You may consider taking written notes, if that helps. The

> "I KNOW THAT YOU BELIEVE YOU UNDERSTAND WHAT YOU THINK I SAID, BUT I'M NOT SURE YOU REALIZE THAT WHAT YOU HEARD IS NOT WHAT I MEANT."
>
> -ROBERT MCCLOSKEY

idea is not to have the customer repeat the same information several times; it may frustrate him or her to a point that he or she sees no benefit in providing further details. Having said that, if you don't understand something that the customer said, by all means do ask for clarification. If the customer is not providing enough information for you to be able to conclude what it is that he or she really needs, then it's time to start thinking like a good pharmacist. I am sure that at some point in time you've visited your pharmacist to get over-the-counter medicine for yourself or for one of your family members. What happened? Pharmacist greeted you and asked, *"How can I help you?"* When we generally visit a pharmacist, we often think that we know what we need. In reality, is that always the case? What I am getting at is that when we ask our pharmacist to give us medicine for a cold, cough, or fever, we think that is *the* problem; whereas it's only the *symptom* of the problem, and not the *root cause*. Any pharmacist can pull a medicine off the shelf and let you go on your way. This medicine will only treat the symptoms giving some temporary relief but it won't even touch the heart of the real problem. On the other hand, a good pharmacist will probe you to really understand the nature of the problem as to when the fever started; is the cough dry or wet; is the nose running and so on.

Upon the diagnosis, this pharmacist may give you something for temporary relief but will also recommend you go see a doctor since it could be an infection that may need a doctor's prescription for the needed antibiotics to kill the bacteria—the root of the problem. Likewise, as a *Customer Service Professional* one may have to ask probing questions to get down to exactly what it is the customer *wants* and more importantly what it is he or she really *needs*.

Rule # 3 – Ask the "right" questions

You may ask, is there is a better way to start probing the customer? Where to begin? What to ask? I guess we all can count the number of letters in the word "**QUESTION**". Yes, there are exactly *eight* in number. Then perhaps there are at least *eight* ways you can probe...

What[1]	*Whose[2]*	*When[3]*	*Who[4]*
Where[5]	*Whom[6]*	*Were[7]*	*Which[8]*

Let's discuss these *8W* in reference to the context; once you see their practical relevance, you can apply them to your own situation. Say a customer is having a problem with her wireless phone so she calls into customer service and says "*I have a problem and I need help*". In order for a *Customer Service Professional* to resolve the issue, probing the customer is a must and this is where *8W* can come handy.

Customer Service Professional: "*What[1] seems to be the problem?*"
Customer: "*I can't make a call. Every time I try to call, I hear a small beep and the call ends. It doesn't even ring*".
[1]*Diagnosis*: There are at least three areas we need to look into (a) *Billing*—to make sure that the wireless service is not suspended for non-payment (b) *Network*—to check if there is any lack of coverage or outage going on at the location where the customer is trying to use the phone (c) *Device*—perhaps something is wrong with the physical phone preventing it from making or receiving calls.

Customer Service Professional: "*I see that you have two phone lines setup on this account. Whose[2] phone is having the problem? Is it just yours or is the other phone having the same issue?*"

Customer: *"It's only my phone causing all the trouble. My husband's phone works just fine, I spoke to him an hour ago using my office phone".*

₂Diagnosis: Looks like there is nothing wrong with the billing i.e. the account is current (up-to-date and fully paid) or else both the phones, being on the same account, would have faced service disruption. Had it been the case i.e. both phones unable to make or receive calls then there would have been a strong possibility that the account is overdue and perhaps suspended for non-payment. If so, a simple account lookup and getting the payment from the customer and bringing the account to current status would have fixed the issue. However, given that the account is already current and it's only the wife facing the problem, the issue could be with the network or the device (not the billing). It is best to connect with this customer over a phone other than her wireless handset for the sake of troubleshooting.

Customer Service Professional: *" **When**[3] was the last time you were successfully able to use the phone before the problem started?"*

Customer: *"Yesterday afternoon it was just fine and I didn't get a chance to use it until this morning only to find that I can't even make a call".*

₃Diagnosis: Looks like something happened within the last 24 hours that triggered the problem so we need to check into anything that might have occurred within this timeframe.

Customer Service Professional: *" **Who**[4] else used your device in the past 24 hours?"*

Customer: *"Well my son borrowed the phone from me yesterday evening".*

₄Diagnosis: There is a possibility that the son might have caused physical damage to the phone that the customer is not aware of. If this can be confirmed then we simply have to replace the physical device and the problem is fixed. If not, we need to probe further.

Customer Service Professional: *" **Where**[5] are you currently located? Could you please provide me with the postal (zip) code or a street address? Are you getting a strong signal, say at least 3 bars on your phone?"*

Customer: *"I am downtown, calling you from my office which is the billing address on my account. I always have strong reception; as a matter of fact, I have five full bars showing on my screen. I never had an issue using my phone at this location".*

₅Diagnosis: Looks like we do have the network coverage or else the customer wouldn't have received strong signals (five bars) on her phone. It is important to consider that network coverage could vary and at times wireless service providers depend on their partner companies to provide accessibility in the areas where they lack their own footprints. In case of lack of coverage, we'd have asked the customer to try to change her location such as getting close to a window to get better reception and that would have resolved the issue or get out of the elevator first and then try to make a call. Maybe the problem could be due to a network outage at the downtown location. Looking up such information in our system or by checking up with the "technical" team will determine if that is the case. If so, let the customer know that though we do have coverage in the area, it's due to a network maintenance/outage (whatever the case may be) that she is unable to call. In addition to an apology for the inconvenience that the customer had to go through, the customer also deserves to know how long this outage may last (if that information is available). We haven't resolved the issue but at least we know the root cause and thus can set appropriate expectations with the customer. What if we find that there are no network issues in the downtown area? I guess we continue to probe.

Customer Service Professional: "**Whom**[6] *are you trying to call? Is it one specific number that you are trying to reach?*"
Customer: *"I have been just trying to reach my friend on her cell phone".*
[6]**Diagnosis**: Perhaps the issue could be with the friend's cell phone instead.

Customer Service Professional: "**Were**[7] *you able to call any other number?*"
Customer: *"No, I haven't tried calling anyone else".*
[7]**Diagnosis**: We can't say for certain whether the issue is with our customer or the other party. Have the customer call a different number. If it works then it looks like the nature of the problem is somehow tied to this one specific number. Now have the customer call her friend using a phone other than her cell phone, say a landline (she would have to put the customer service professional on hold while attempting to reach her friend using the landline phone). If the call still doesn't go through then we know it's the friend's device or service having the issue, not our customer's. What if the customer is unable to call using her cell phone no matter which number she dials; moreover, she is able to reach her friend using a landline? In that case, our hunt for the root cause of the problem continues.

Customer Service Professional: "**Which**[8] *cell phone device are you using? Can you please provide the make and the model number?*"
Customer: *"Not sure, I got it as a gift from someone last month".*
[8]**Diagnosis**: There could be a known manufacturer's defect or a recall for the exact type of phone that the customer is using. You may wonder why bother asking the customer. Shouldn't we look up such information by pulling the customer's account? Well, at times customers switch their phones without informing their cell phone service providers (removing the SIM card from the *old* phone and putting it into the *new* one) so the customer account information may not be up-to-date. We can ask the customer to find the information on the make and the model underneath the battery (for most cell phone devices). Once we know which phone it is, we can search our systems to see if there is any known defect for the exact make and model and also if there is a recall issued for it. If so, getting the handset replaced will resolve the issue. By the way, I personally once encountered

an unusual issue when a handset with a specific make and model prevented a customer from making outgoing calls within a certain area code. There was a known defect and a recall was issued where and the device had to be replaced.

Now that you can see how the *8W* can be helpful in probing the customer, you can apply them using your discretion. I am not recommending that we ask all eight questions to every customer. All I am suggesting is that if you're not sure where to begin then give a couple of these *8W* a try to kick off the probing process. By the way, did you notice the two things that are common in all eight questions? Yes, they all start with the letter *W*. That was easy! What about the other one? Aren't they all *open-ended* questions (as opposed to *closed-ended*) that force the customer to answer you with something other than

> "IT IS BETTER TO ASK SOME OF THE QUESTIONS THAN TO KNOW ALL OF THE ANSWERS"
>
> -JAMES THURBER

just a *Yes* or a *No*? Asking open-ended questions wisely plays a key factor in gathering all the pertinent information to get to the root cause of any issue!

Rule # 4 – Break all communication barriers

How to tackle language barriers

Language differences can be a major obstacle in the communication process. In today's multicultural and multilingual society, it is increasingly essential for those in customer service to have the skills to overcome lingo blockade and to converse effectively with those who may not be as fluent in speaking English. **Communication is a "two-way" street.** If you try to tell something to a customer in a face-to-face conversation, and in response the customer simply smiles and nods at everything you say, but neither asks a question nor expresses an opinion or concern, it should ring a bell that there is a possible communication gap. In a telephonic conversation, such a customer

> "IF WE SPOKE A DIFFERENT LANGUAGE, WE WOULD PERCEIVE A SOMEWHAT DIFFERENT WORLD."
>
> -LUDWIG WITTGENSTEIN

may respond with a *Yes* regardless of whether you ask a question or provide information.

Here are the five strategies (tried and tested—they do work) to help you overcome language barriers:

1) Speak slowly ... but not loudly—please keep in mind that such customers may face language difficulty, but do not have any hearing problems.

2) Use Visual Aids ... to supplement your verbal explanation such as displaying actual product samples and going through brochures with graphics when dealing with the customer face-to-face. If the customer is being helped over the phone, check if the customer has access to a computer with the Internet connection. If so, have the customer browse to the webpage that contains the information that you are trying to explain so the visual can complement the auditory. If the customer can also be directed to a video posted on your company's website or on a social media site, even better, since the video can be played over and over. This really helps when trying to explain something that is technical or complex in nature. If that is not possible then see if the customer can visit one of your company's stores and get help in person. Same tips will also apply for online customer service such as chat sessions.

3) Avoid Gobbledygook ... by staying away from the use of technical terminologies, industry jargon, and slang. This type of talk can confuse just about anyone, let alone someone with a language barrier. It's best to keep all conversation in plain layperson's terms.

4) Grab the "key" words ... when you talk to the customer, you may not be able to understand the entire phrase due to the language affair. However, try to pick up the key words the customer is trying to say e.g. "phone no battery" or "$100 discount". Then put those words into the context of the type of service or product you offer, including any sales or promotions presently being offered. Once you have an idea of what the customer needs, check your understanding by paraphrasing what you heard back to the customer, using a closed-ended question – again one that can only be answered in either a *Yes* or a *No,* e.g. *"So just to reconfirm what you are asking ....is that right?"* This is to ensure that you have in fact understood the customer's concern.

5) Get help from family or a friend ... who can represent your customer as last resort. Many organizations have started providing customer service in two or more languages, for example many U.S. companies are supporting customers in both English and Spanish. Likewise, most Canadian firms are assisting clients in English as well as French. If that's the case, we can simply transfer the customer over to our colleagues who speak his or her language. What if we don't have the luxury of having multilingual support in the language that the customer is comfortable with and you've tried everything you can but there are still communication gaps? As mentioned above, only as the last resort, you may want to consider speaking to someone else in the family who can communicate the customer's side of the story to you. Your customer may not be able to converse fluently in English; however, that may not necessarily be the case for the rest of the customer's family members such as kids who could be more conversant in English than their parents, and they can help you out. It doesn't have to be someone from the family; a friend or a colleague can also lend a hand. Regardless, I can't emphasize enough the importance of having the consent of the customer as well as your own organization *before* taking this route due to privacy and liability concerns.

By the way, for online consumer support, you can also take advantage of language translation software that allows you to send an email or chat by typing your text in English, while your customer will receive your message in his or her native language. With the advancement in software engineering, you can now also have your voice conversation (spoken works) translated from one language to another, real time. If your organization has a large multilingual customer base and language barrier is causing an on-going communication breakdown, then investing in such technologies is worth looking into!

How to handle limitations due to impairment (hearing, speech, visual)

Hearing Impairment: What about the customers who have hearing problems? In this situation, our speech should not only be slow and clear but we also have to speak up a little bit for face-to-face customer service. Otherwise the tips discussed above can be equally effective in assisting those with auditory limitations. For non face-to-face customer service, many organizations provide service through a special device called a Teletypewriter or Telecommunications Display Device (TTY / TDD). This is a text telephone or related computer program that works through a teletype system. We should take advantage of these services to overcome communication barriers and to provide superior quality customer service, if available.

Speech Impairment: As for communicating to the customers, who have speech impairments, you might want to avoid asking too many open-ended questions or else they will have a hard time explaining their point of view; closed-ended questions work better. Interrupting the customer and putting words in his or her mouth will not help but hurt. Not only can it be offensive but also it prevents the customer from expressing the concerns from his or her own perspective. Let the customer take the time to speak while we listen patiently and carefully, taking mental notes or jotting down the key points on a piece of paper because the last thing we want to do is to have such customers repeat everything all over. The Teletypewriter or Telecommunications Display Device (TTY / TDD) service mentioned above can also apply to those with speech impairments.

Visual Impairment: Providing a face-to-face or over-the-phone customer service to those with visual impairment can be more effective if we rely more on our verbal explanation rather than referring them to printed material when explaining our products or services, unless the information being shared is available in *Braille*. When assisting these customers over the Internet, say using a chat session, make sure to adjust font size accordingly. If directing these customers to our website, it is important that the website is compliant with accessibility standards; *screen reader* computer software can effectively read only those websites that are designed accordingly. There is lots of information on this subject available on the Internet; a simple search using keyword, *web accessibility,* will direct you to the relevant links.

Activity 7 – Bridge the gap

Share your experience within the group where you had a difficult time understanding a customer's concerns. Where was the communication *gap*? How did you *deal* with it? Is there anything you could have done *differently* to handle the situation better?

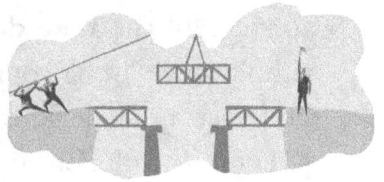

Important: Please be mindful that such a discussion can be sensitive in nature. Use discretion when mentioning any type of handicap, language, or culture barriers. The idea is simply to share and learn but without being indifferent to others.

Activity 8 – Solve the problem

Connect **all the nine dots** (see the illustration below) by drawing only **four straight** lines without once lifting your pencil (avoid a pen, so if needed you can erase and retry it) from the paper, nor tracing over any line that you've already drawn. By the way, it's not a trick question—a solution to the problem does exist. Take your time but if you give up, please feel free to look up the answer on the Internet; just type *"how to connect nine dots with four lines"* in one of the search engines—Google, Yahoo, or Bing—and then click on the *Images* link on the menu bar. Please don't proceed further unless you either solve the problem yourself or at least familiarize yourself with the solution available on the web.

Note: This activity is meant to be done individually, not in a group.

III – RESEARCH SOLUTION

Once assured that we have indeed understood our customer's concerns, our next step is to find a solution that actually works!

Tip # 1: Think Outside The Box

Let me share with you a real call that came into customer service where the customer was looking for a cell phone with some specific features meant for those with hearing impairment. The *Customer Service Professional* who took the call looked up but couldn't find any such device available in the warehouse inventory where the phones are shipped from. She could have just apologized for not being able to provide what the customer was looking for and leave it at that. Nothing more was required of her other than checking the online warehouse inventory. Instead, she started researching online to find all the devices designed specifically for those with hearing impairment. After short listing a few of the devices that met the customer's needs best, she further researched all wireless stores located within a reasonable driving distance from where the customer resided. Then she started calling each of those stores to see if any one of them carries one of those specific cell phones. Guess what? She did find this one store carrying just one of the devices that were shortlisted. She provided the customer with the name of the store, address, store hours, and contact number. In addition, she also informed the customer about the make, model, and the cost of the wireless device that was readily available at the store. *Way to Go* for thinking outside the box!

> "NO PROBLEM CAN STAND THE ASSAULT OF SUSTAINED THINKING."
>
> -VOLTAIRE

No one prefers a cookie cutter approach. Customers are demanding solutions that are tailored to their specific needs. This is why ensuring you understand customers' needs is a critical prerequisite to researching the right solution for them. If you know a solution that exactly meet their needs, then your job has become so much easier—just offer them the solution—the product or service that will make them happy and satisfied. You're done! However, at times you simply don't have a solution available—all you know is the nature of the problem. For example, a customer who has lost his cell phone, calls into customer service and asks for a phone replacement—demanding a $500.00 smart phone with all the bells and whistles—but is not prepared to sign any new service contract or willing to spend a penny over $100.00. To make things worse, he doesn't have any insurance on his account that could have paid for the replacement device. OK, so we do know the customer's demands but what if we aren't in a position to offer this $500.00 phone for anything less, unless the customer signs a new service contract? What do we do now?

Tip # 2: Focus on the solution—not the problem

Continuing with the above example, we can get to a point where we don't know how to move forward; it's probably a good time to take a step back and revisit *Ensure Understanding*. Find out why the customer is so keen on getting this $500.00 smart phone. Say through probing we find out that the only reason the customer is asking for this specific phone is because of watching an advertisement on TV. Further inquiry reveals that the customer uses the cell phone just to make and receive calls, doesn't even go onto the Internet and sure doesn't need all the advanced features that come with this smart phone in question. As we look into the options available, we find a phone for as little as $49.99 that has

> "ASK YOUR CUSTOMERS TO BE PART OF THE SOLUTION, AND DON'T VIEW THEM AS PART OF THE PROBLEM."
>
> -ALAN WEISS

practically everything the customer wants and for half the price that the customer is willing to pay. Comparing and explaining the choices available, there is a good chance that the customer will buy into taking an option that will work for him without spending a fortune, leaving him satisfied and content. In addition, now it's a good time to also offer insurance to provide coverage for any future incidents. Long story short, an "acceptable" solution that is practical is far better than the pursuit of an "ideal" resolution that can't be achieved.

Tip # 3: Don't Prejudge – Rather Research

Allow me to elaborate on this tip by sharing with you (as crazy as it may sound) a **true story** that was posted on the *University of Waterloo* website but that I originally learned when I was training *Customer Service Professionals* for Nissan North America. **It's about a customer who claimed that his car is allergic to vanilla ice-cream.**

A complaint was received by the Pontiac Division of General Motors:

"This is the second time I have written you, and I don't blame you for not answering me, because I kind of sounded crazy, but it is a fact that we have a tradition in our family of ice cream for dessert after dinner each night. But the kind of ice cream varies so, every night, after we've eaten the whole family votes on which kind of ice cream we should have and I drive down to the store to get it. It's also a fact that I recently purchased a new Pontiac and since then my trips to the store have created a problem.

You see, every time I buy vanilla ice cream, when I start back from the store my car won't start. If I get any other kind of ice cream, the car starts just fine. I want you to know I'm serious about this question, no matter how silly it sounds: 'What is there about a Pontiac that makes it not start when I get vanilla ice cream, and easy to start whenever I get any other kind?'"

The Pontiac President was understandably sceptical about the letter, but sent an engineer to check it out anyway. The latter was surprised to be greeted by a successful, obviously well-educated man in a fine neighbourhood. He had arranged to meet the man just after dinner time, so the two hopped into the car and drove to the ice cream store. It was vanilla ice cream that night and, sure enough, after they came back to the car, it wouldn't start.

The engineer returned for three more nights. The first night, the man got chocolate. The car started. The second night, he got strawberry. The car started. The third night he ordered vanilla. The car failed to start.

Now the engineer, being a logical man, refused to believe that this man's car was allergic to vanilla ice cream. He arranged, therefore, to continue his visits for as long as it took to solve the problem. And toward this end he began to take notes: he jotted down all sorts of data, time of day, type of gas used, time to drive back and forth, etc.

In a short time, he had a clue: the man took less time to buy vanilla than any other flavour. Why? The answer was in the layout of the store.

Vanilla, being the most popular flavour, was in a separate case at the front of the store for quick pickup. All the other flavours were kept in the back of the store at a different counter where it took considerably longer to find the flavour and get checked out.

Now the question for the engineer was why the car wouldn't start when it took less time. Once time became the problem – not the vanilla ice cream – the engineer quickly came up with the answer: vapour lock. It was happening every night, but the extra time taken to get the other flavours allowed the engine to cool down sufficiently to start. When the man got vanilla, the engine was still too hot for the vapour lock to dissipate."

Moral of the story: Even insane-looking problems are sometimes real and deserve your attention.

Interesting? Isn't it? Kudos to the president of the Pontiac Division, who chose not to prejudge, rather researched—separating facts from fiction—and found the solution to the problem.

"IT IS HARDER TO CRACK A PREJUDICE THAN AN ATOM."

-ALBERT EINSTEIN

IV - VALUE TIME

Unlike money, when it comes to time, the richest person in the world to the poorest of all has no choice but to spend it at the pace of 60 minutes per hour and 24 hours a day—No more, No less! You can neither buy it nor bank it; perhaps this is why time is so valued. We like to spend it where it's most beneficial whether personally, financially, or otherwise. How often do we drop by our favourite pizza shop just to thank them for their on-time delivery and great tasting hot pizza every time we order one? Who among us has picked up the phone to call customer service to say a good word for providing a trouble-free landline home telephone service that

> "ONE THING YOU CAN'T RECYCLE IS WASTED TIME."
>
> -UNKNOWN

never drops our calls? When was the last time we emailed our bank appreciating their online banking system that saves us both time and hassle? If you are like most people, you may have done it on rare occasions in your lifetime or perhaps never, and this is the norm. Why? Well, don't we have better things to do in life with our time than showing gratitude for a service that is supposed to be flawless in the first place, after all we've paid for it—it wasn't free! So when do we generally get in touch with our service providers? Well, when there is a problem!

Setting the expectations

So imagine if Mrs. Smith who is already unhappy about her utility bill being higher than she expected; but on top of that, now she has to spend (read: **waste**) her time with someone over the phone to get the issue resolved. This is where we need to be especially considerate of her valuable time and provide the solution as quickly as we can. The least we should do is to set realistic expectations as to how long it will take us to resolve the billing problem. Have you or someone you know ever called in to your Internet service provider that you can't get online? These types of issues may take a little more time than say changing one's cell phone voicemail access code. It's difficult to put a definite time tag for a job that requires some serious troubleshooting, simply because the underlying reason is unknown and needs to be investigated.

This is where we should draw upon our own past experiences and on the advice of the *Subject Matter Experts* (SMEs) in our organization who may have dealt with similar situations, to get an idea how long it will take us to resolve the issue in order to set proper expectations with our customer as a respect for his or her time. The last thing we should do is to start researching a solution without engaging our customer in what we're doing. Say troubleshooting an Internet connection issue may require us to ask our customer several questions such as: *When* did the problem start? *What* happens as you launch your Internet browser? *Which* type of modem are you using? (Remember the **8W** we discussed earlier). Before we jump into asking these questions, it's best that we first let the customer know how we are going to approach the issue at hand, that it may take some time and most importantly, get the customer's blessing if she is willing to spend that time with us, at this very moment. For example, *"Mrs. Smith, we apologize for the inconvenience, I am going to be asking you a series of questions and if you could please stay with me over the phone as I may also ask you to change some of your computer settings. From past experiences, depending on the problem, it may take anywhere from 15 to 45 minutes, before we can get your Internet up and running. Shall we proceed?"* This way, the customer knows up front that it could take as long as 45 minutes before she is off the hook. What if she is expecting an important call soon? If so, she may decide to deal with this matter later. If so, we can offer the customer a call back when she is available.

Once I took my family to one of our favourite seafood restaurants. As soon as I stepped in, a lady at the reception advised me how busy they were and that it would take at least an hour before they'd have any seating available. Even though I decided to take my family elsewhere that evening, I'll go back to that restaurant anytime. I wouldn't have been impressed if I had to wait in line for 20 minutes, only to find out that I'd have to wait for another 40—my time was valued.

Counting every minute

When it comes to respecting someone's time, even little things can matter. For face-to-face customer service, while checking-in a customer at a hotel, one notices that there is another customer waiting in line, simply saying, *"I will be with you momentarily"*, making the customer feel acknowledged. As for over-the-phone customer service, say in call/contact centers, it's highly recommended that based on the current call volume, the Interactive Voice Response (IVR) system should inform each customer who is calling in of the average waiting time to connect to a live person. Moreover, while the customer is on hold, Interactive Voice Response systems should be programmed to inform the automated ways to say *checking up on the account balance* or *taking payment* in order to save time. Whereas for the online customer service, time expectations can be setup by having a window pop up advising the customer of the estimated remaining time before connecting to the live chat session for customer support.

Offering additional assistance

Once the customer issue is dealt with, be sure to offer additional assistance to the customer. For example, *"Mrs. Smith, is there is anything else I can help you with?"* You want to ensure that when you end the interaction with your customer, all of the customer's issues are resolved, not just the one that was brought up in the first place. You don't want your customer to go back into the waiting line to get any secondary issue resolved, only because he or she forgot to mention it when getting the primary one taken care of. Your goal should be to achieve **"one contact resolution"** by addressing all of the customer's issues the first time he or she gets in touch with you. The customer should not have to reach out (face-to-face, over-the-phone, online) again.

Remember the old cliché, *Time is Money*. Perhaps it's worth even more—money not spent well can be gained back which is definitely not the case with time!

Activity 9 – Time savings

Please come up with a few ways that you and your organization can save your customer's time or set proper time delay expectations. Which one do you think will be the most beneficial and why? Share and compare your list with your colleagues.

V - INFORM OPTIONS

When I was growing up as a kid and wanted to get a pop – the only two options I had were either Coke or Pepsi. There was no such thing as Coca-Cola Zero, Caffeine-Free Coca-Cola, and Cherry Coke. Likewise, Pepsi Lime Soft Drink, Pepsi Max Soft Drink, and Pepsi Caffeine Free brand names were unheard of during my childhood. Today, we can't even imagine a grocery store carrying only one brand of cereal or visualize an electronic store carrying all TVs of the same size. Visit any paint shop to get *white* paint and you get a wide selection to choose from. Is it *Eggshell* or *Flat*? Do you prefer *Gloss* or *Semi-Gloss*? How about *Snow White*? Since today's customers are demanding more than ever, customer service ought to be geared up

> "INFORMATION CAN BRING YOU CHOICES AND CHOICES BRING POWER - EDUCATE YOURSELF ABOUT YOUR OPTIONS AND CHOICES. NEVER REMAIN IN THE DARK OF IGNORANCE."
>
> -JOY PAGE

to inform them of their options. Again, first and foremost, we must have done a good job way back in the *Ensure Understanding* phase; only then are we in the best position to advise our customers of the most appropriate alternatives to make the right decision. After ensuring that you understand a customer's needs and wants, you may realize that you have more than one option that may fulfill a customer's requirements. This is where the customer needs to be fully educated about all the different routes he or she can take when it comes to making a judgement as to what is the best for him or her.

Though businesses offer a variety (and they should), it's the *Customer Service Professional's* job to inform the limited number of options that meet the customer needs best. Say a customer visits a store to purchase a computer and asks for help. Most electronic stores carry dozens of brands. It won't do any good to the customer if one was to provide a list of all the 35 computers—desktops, laptops, and tablets—they carry and ask the customer to pick one. If choosing a computer would have been that simple and straightforward, why would any customer bother to drop into a store? Why not just buy it by visiting an online auction website (perhaps for a lesser price)? On the other hand, it's even worse if we simply offer the latest and greatest computer to a customer who only plans to use it for email and simple Internet browsing. However, it doesn't mean we offer the cheapest one, either.

So if offering everything we have is not going to help, and promoting the most expensive one or selling the cheapest one is also not always the best option for the customer, what should we do?

The Human Element

Customers seek options that fit their needs best and ones from which they can get the best value for their money. Some websites try to do similar (artificial) thinking and ask customers questions and based upon the responses, they propose solutions. We, the *Customer Service Professionals*, with human (real) intelligence can do far better than any software programming. Even though artificial intelligence has its own merit, it can never replace the human element.

Unlike software code that responds in a cut and dry manner like an *if-then* logic, the human brain is capable of doing a lot more! For online or over-the-phone customer service, one can quickly pull up a customer account history—checking out notes left on the account based on earlier interactions with the customer—and see if there have been any trends that could lead us to better understand where the customer is coming from based on past experiences. If speaking to a customer, our mind can also detect the hidden messages coming from the customer's tone of voice. In a face-to-face situation, our intelligence can also read the body language, making sound judgements every step of the way during customer service. How well is a customer taking the options that are provided to him or her; not only how he or she thinks about the choices being offered rationally, but also how he or she feels about them, emotionally.

Objection vis-à-vis Rejection

Moreover, every time you offer the customer an option, you may encounter an objection. Please be aware that an *objection* is not the same as a *rejection*. Simply put, rejection is where the customer makes it loud and clear that he or she is not interested in your offer, period. Especially if it's coming from **I KNOW** customer (remember *8i*). It is going to be counterproductive to indulge in (again: Value Time) discussing an option that is rejected by the customer. On the other hand, an objection is where the customer has interest, yet some hesitation. It's like saying, *"I would have considered this option **but**."* This is where customer service comes in to remove those obstacles from the way by further educating customers about the decision they are reluctant to make. This will ensure that when the customer does choose one of the options that are offered, it's well informed, well understood, and well accepted.

Customer makes the final call

One should always let the customer make a final decision out of multiple options rather than providing them with a solo choice to make. In case something goes wrong later, the customer can't then come back to haunt you as if you forced them to take that one and only option that you offered. No manufacturer or service provider can come up with a product or a service with zero-defects—things can go wrong. We don't live in a perfect world, do we?

Bottom line, never impose your preferences on the customer; our job is to inform the best options given the needs and wants of the customer and let him or her make the final call.

Activity 10 – Artificial intelligence

Do you see your customers benefiting from the use of a software application with artificial intelligence that will help them make better decisions and select better choices for themselves? Is it worth investing in such technologies? What are the pros and cons?

VI - CONFIRM MUTUAL AGREEMENT

Now that you have informed the customer of the best possible options, what's next? Shall we expect the customer to simply pick one of the choices being offered at face value and accept it? We're close but not quite there, yet! Really, how many of us go through each and every fine print when signing a contract with our wireless service provider? Seriously, do we know of anyone who went through the entire warranty booklet—cover to cover—when buying a new vehicle? Honestly, how many of us take the time to read and understand before clicking on the option to accept the terms and conditions when installing software on our computer? The vast majority of consumers skip this part and end up locking themselves into an agreement without even knowing the ins and outs of it. Maybe they don't want to take the time to go through the dry and boring clauses that are probably put together by some legal experts. Instead, they just can't wait to start reaping the benefits of what they just got—start texting their friends with their neat looking smart phone; take their family or friends for a ride in their cool looking dream car; start working on the project that required the software that they just installed. The bottom line is that customers are often unaware of the terms they agree to and it is our job as *Customer Service Professionals* to educate them with integrity and honesty on what they need to know before they accept the offer. Furthermore, if the customer likes to place some pre-conditions before making the purchase (something very common in real estate transactions), we must look into them and confirm with the customer (preferably in writing) if we can accept them or not—I call this entire process, *Confirm Mutual Agreement*.

> "UNLESS BOTH SIDES WIN, NO AGREEMENT CAN BE PERMANENT."
>
> -JIMMY CARTER

Once I was opening a bank account; as you can expect, I didn't care to read all those terms and conditions and was almost ready to sign the dotted line when my banker stopped me. He wanted me to make sure that I understood the implications of an important clause in the contract – one I must have ignored as I skimmed through the agreement. He pointed out a phrase which stated that in case of a discrepancy in the account balance that shows up on my monthly bank statement, I only have 30 days to dispute, i.e. say my account balance is $1000.00, and I receive a bank statement indicating it's only $100.00. Unless I dispute the missing $900.00 within a month, the bank is not going to be liable to reimburse the amount. Though I didn't like the policy, I was okay with setting up the account since I was educated on the agreement *before* I signed it—the gentleman at the bank came up with a "full disclosure" of what was at stake.

Oftentimes, we tend to ignore such key points buried somewhere in the written agreements and get to know them only when we've got a problem. It certainly does no good to a customer if he or she learns about the terms *after* he or she signs an accord. It is our responsibility as a *Customer Service Professional* to go through with the customer the terms and limitations of our products or service. It's our job to understand and document the customer's pre-conditions and make sure there is a confirmation of mutual agreement between both parties, before any contract is signed, regardless of whether it's done verbally, electronically, or on-paper. Please be advised that by no means am I suggesting reading the entire service contract or a warranty manual, word for word, with your customer. All I am saying is that we may know a fine print about our service contract or product warranty that in our opinion is critical for the customer (like the example of the banker) so we should make it a point the customer is aware of it before making a commitment.

The fact of the matter is that most potential customers are attracted toward our products and services because of the exciting benefits they can reap to make their life simple, better, or fun! Having to understand all the terms and conditions that go along with those products and services is seldom a matter of priority. At the same time, we being in the customer service business know very well the frequent reasons customers call us back complaining about the limitations they face when using our product and services but were never informed of in the first place. So don't you think that at times the complaints we get from our customers are justified because not only do they face problems that they never expected, but also they were never cautioned of such potential issues at the time when they signed up for our service or purchased our product?

For example, the *Customer Service Professionals* serving the wireless industry should inform customers not only about the cool features of the slim and thin touch screen device but also if and why the first bill is expected to be higher than a regular (subsequent) bill due to extra charges such as account activation, accessories cost, advanced billing etc. Explain what sort of prorated charges (if any) they'll see on that first bill and why. Explain what it means to be in one's home calling area as opposed to being roaming and the charges associated with such usage. Talk about dropped calls, dead zones and perhaps most importantly the limitations associated with their coverage and the fact that no wireless company, no matter how good the network, can guarantee full service (both voice and data), 100% of the time, at all locations across the country. On the other hand, if a customer says I need you to waive my one-time setup fee, check your policy to see if you can actually do it. If you can and are willing to offer this deal to the customer then make sure that it's well documented and well communicated to anyone who needs to know, so that there is left no doubt regarding what was mutually agreed.

As another example, for those who are serving the auto industry and helping people make the second major purchase of their lives (besides buying a home) not only should you take customer for a test drive, but also on "an agreement drive". In plain English, clarify to the customer all the terms of agreement that is part of the warranty coverage that comes with each new vehicle. First of all put in plain words what exactly the warranty covers—a defect in material and workmanship during the coverage period. When you say that they have nothing to worry about for the next 60 months or 60,000 miles, make sure you qualify your statement by adding **whichever occurs first**. Help the customer understand the difference between various categories of warranty such as Basic, Power Train, Emission, Battery, Tires, Accessories and so forth and the fact that coverage across these multiple categories (in most cases) does differ. Make sure there is no ambiguity whether towing, car rental, and roadside assistance is covered under the manufacturer's warranty or if the customer has to pay extra for it. If the customer asks for free oil changes for the next 6 months, make sure you let the customer know (in black and white) whether you agree to it or not. Again, putting the mutual agreement in writing is a sound business practice.

By the way, the basic principles of customer service discussed here apply equally to those who are in project management and consulting businesses regardless of the industry such as Information Technology, Aerospace, Construction, Business Process Outsourcing, Industrial, you name it. Any decent size project costs companies millions (if not billions) so there is a lot that is at stake. Make sure that the *Service Level Agreement* (SLA) has incorporated all the details with regards to any change in the scope, timeline, or cost of the project. Most importantly what would be the "sign-off criteria" deciding whether the final deliverable is what was expected and promised? If clients like

> "CUSTOMER SERVICE IS NOT A DEPARTMENT, IT'S EVERYONE'S JOB."
>
> -UNKNOWN

to impose any penalties say for missing the deadline or being unable to meet any part of the *Service Level Agreement*, it must be documented and communicated to all concerned parties before reaching any agreement. Higher standards of customer service require an open and constant communication throughout the different phases of the project from planning to analysis, design to testing and finally the implementation. It's only then that we can succeed to reach higher customer satisfaction.

To sum up, it's the job of a *Customer Service Professional* to confirm that "key" terms and conditions, both explicit and implicit, are **discussed, defined** and **documented (3D)** *before* a mutual agreement takes place, so the customer can expect to get exactly what was established, nothing less!

Activity 11 – Discuss, Define, Document *(3D)*

(a) List a couple of points that you believe are critical and should be *discussed* with your customers before any commitments are made on either side with regards to your products or services.

(b) What do you think is the best way to *define* any pre-conditions brought forth by your customer and agreed to by you so it could be easily referenced by anyone else in your organization at a later time in case there is a dispute or confusion?

(c) Which medium is more appropriate to *document* your confirmed mutual agreement—electronically or on paper?

VII - EXCEED EXPECTATIONS

Doesn't it seem that we've already done enough for our customers? What else is there? You know what? The truth of the matter is that so far all we have done (though critical and crucial) is the bare minimum of what is expected from us in the first place and nothing more! Don't we all expect to be treated with courtesy; that others will listen and understand our concerns; that someone will look into a solution to our problem; respect our time; inform us of our options; and clarify any terms or conditions so we don't have any surprises later? But what else then needs to be done? Well, let's go back to one of the **3C—Competition** that we discussed under the topic, *Why Customer Service*, at the beginning of this book. Don't you think that our competitors will also be striving for the same level of service vis-à-vis what we are trying to do for the customer – meet the customer's expectations? So what can be done to *out-do* our competition? The answer is to *Exceed Expectations*—go beyond the call of duty! That leads us into our next question and that is *how*?

> "THERE ARE NO TRAFFIC JAMS ALONG THE EXTRA MILE."
>
> -ROGER STAUBACH

Do you play cards? I don't. But if I ask one (who is good at it) the significance of the Aces when playing a game, the common response I get is that having the Aces (depending on the game) will put one in a stronger position over the opponent. Likewise, in the game of *Customer Service*, you'll also need the Aces to have an edge over your competitor. Let us call them *3A*. They are **(1) Advise (2) Assure (3) Appreciate.**

Advise

What do "excellent" doctors and tax consultants have in common? They both provide "beneficial" advice that can only come from a subject matter expert. What do we expect when we visit a doctor? Well, we expect a doctor to diagnose the health issue and prescribe the appropriate medicine. Whereas, an exceptional doctor will do more (read: exceed expectations) by advising us how to live a healthy life style so we don't run into health problems in the future. This reminds me of the adage, "*An ounce of prevention is worth a pound of cure*". What do we expect when we to go to a tax consultant when filing our tax returns? Well, a tax consultant is expected to file our tax returns accurately and on time. Whereas a very good tax consultant will go one step further (again: exceed expectations) by analyzing our financial situation and advising us how to minimize our taxes and maximize our returns through proper financial planning.

> "IT'S MUCH HARDER TO PROVIDE A GREAT CUSTOMER SERVICE THAN I WOULD HAVE EVER REALIZED. IT'S MUCH MORE ART THAN SCIENCE IN SOME OF THESE OTHER AREAS AND NOT JUST ABOUT THE FACTS BUT ABOUT HOW YOU ARE CONVEYING THEM."
>
> -DAVID YU

Likewise, what do we expect when we call into customer service to pay our monthly wireless bill? I guess anyone can take our payment to bring our balance to current. However, a good *Customer Service Professional* will try to go above and beyond. This *Customer Service Professional* will take our consent to look through the account to see if we are setup with the right plan at the best price. *"Mr. Smith, your payment has been successfully accepted and your account is now fully current, do you mind if I take a quick look at your account to make sure that you are on the best plan given your current usage? It will only take me a couple of minutes."* For example, a customer is setup on a $40.00 monthly plan that gets him or her 450 *daytime* (also known as *anytime* or *peak-time*) minutes a month. Say as per the plan, any overage (going over the given 450 limit during the *daytime* hours such as between 9:00 a.m. – 6:00 p.m.) is charged at 45¢ for every extra minute on call. Looking through the account, the *Customer Service Professional* finds that the customer is paying over $100.00 a month (despite being on a $40.00 monthly plan). Further investigation reveals that customer average daytime usage is around 600 minutes and as a result he is incurring extra charges on an on-going basis (600-450=150; 150*45¢=$67.50). The *Customer Service Professional* will take the time to educate and advise the customer that given the average usage of *daytime* minutes over the last six months is around the 600 mark, it's better to switch to the next plan that will cost say $60.00 a month, paying only $20.00 over the current plan, but in return offer say 900 *daytime* minutes which will put a stop to any overage charge on the monthly basis. Not to mention, the customer will have an extra 300 minutes in case he needs them. This change will result in an on-going savings of no less than $50.00 a month, taking the taxes into consideration.

This beneficial advice will *prevent* the customer from exceeding his minutes, but will *allow* the *Customer Service Professional* to exceed the expectations. We should seize every opportunity where our *advice* can make a difference!

Assure

To exceed expectations, we as *Customer Service Professionals* need to *assure* our customers that they are getting more than what they expect. In other words, we offer them something of "pure benefit" that they neither demanded nor anticipated. Not only that, our customer should be able to *see* that what is being offered to them is truly advantageous—a valuable giveaway—at no extra cost. However, we must realize that every customer is different; what will work for one, will not work for another. Moreover, what did work for a customer last time may not necessarily have the same impact on a different occasion. Since each customer situation is unique, we need to use our "creative judgement" to offer exciting deals to our customers on an on-going basis; without innovative thinking, we will quickly run out of ideas. This is where the *Think Outside The Box* approach we discussed earlier can come handy.

> "HERE IS A SIMPLE BUT POWERFUL RULE: ALWAYS GIVE PEOPLE MORE THAN WHAT THEY EXPECT TO GET".
>
> -NELSON BOSWELL

If you plan to offer your customer something of monetary value (at no additional charge), it doesn't have to be big, something that will put your business in economic distress. Offering something even simple can be seen as a **great savings** by a customer but will only incur a **small cost** to your business. For example, a free car oil change service can be seen as a $40.00 worth of savings for a customer; however, it will not even cost the business half that amount. As another example, a cellular company giving away a free cell phone can be seen as a savings of $100.00 (assuming that's how the phone is priced in the market); however, it may cost the company only a fraction of that cost given the volume discount wireless companies get from manufacturers. Perhaps you can apply a similar approach to your own line-of-business by offering this "great deal" to your customer, which will result in high savings or satisfaction for your customer but incur minimal or no cost to your business. In return you will gain many years of repeat business. By the way, you don't always have to present something of pecuniary value to exceed customer's expectations. Once, during my stay at a hotel, I asked the front desk lady for a nearby convenience store. All I expected was to get some verbal directions. However, she took the time to go online and provided me with handwritten directions, the name of the store and the store hours. She did more than I asked for—she exceeded my expectations. The minimum we should do is to **assure that our customers have the necessary information that is easy to understand and apply** to get the most out of our product or service and know where to get help if needed—providing our customers with verbal instructions, visual product demonstrations, "how to" guide, user manual, links to relevant websites, contact information (phone, fax, email), and business hours.

Appreciate

How many times have you felt that you were not appreciated even though you chose to give your business to someone? Unfortunately this lack of gratitude toward customers is so common that many customers do *not* even expect a word of thanks in return anymore. This is why when we *do* appreciate, we *do* exceed expectations. It doesn't even cost a penny to say, "*Thank you, we appreciate your business*". Yet, it can have

> "A CUSTOMER IS THE MOST IMPORTANT VISITOR ON OUR PREMISES; HE IS NOT DEPENDENT ON US. WE ARE DEPENDENT ON HIM. HE IS NOT AN INTERRUPTION IN OUR WORK. HE IS THE PURPOSE OF IT. HE IS NOT AN OUTSIDER IN OUR BUSINESS. HE IS PART OF IT. WE ARE NOT DOING HIM A FAVOR BY SERVING HIM. HE IS DOING US A FAVOR BY GIVING US AN OPPORTUNITY TO DO SO".
>
> -GANDHI

a deep impact on our customers. It's like letting them know that we do *not* take our customers for granted. Doing so, in essence, you're saying that it's a privilege to serve you as our customer and we are grateful that even though you could have taken your business elsewhere, you decided to stay with us. According to one survey, what employees valued most from their employer was not higher salaries or compensation. You must have guessed; it was *employee appreciation* that was regarded even higher than *financial reward*. Now imagine how your customers are going to value your business when they get a true sense of appreciation from you? In short, in today's competitive economy, we need to strive, not only to meet but to exceed our customer's expectations to win our customers for good!

Activity 12 – Applying Aces

Describe a situation where you were able to apply any of the *3A* to exceed your customer's expectations. Which of the *3A* do you think can generally have the biggest impact on a customer? In other words, is any one more important than the other? Please discuss among your colleagues.

VIII - ESTABLISH LONG-TERM RELATIONSHIP

How to establish a long-term bond

If I argue that a customer's expectations do not change with time, will it hold any ground, whatsoever? Not likely! Change is an inevitable fact of life that has the power to transform one's needs and wants, financial situation, career, interests, behaviour, habits, attitude, perception, family responsibilities, taste—both likes and dislikes; this list goes on. Change in any of the factors mentioned here can likely transform our customers' expectations too. Even though today we are successful in exceeding our customers' expectations, tomorrow we may fail to even meet them; unless we make an effort to establish this customer relationship! We really can't afford to lose our customers, can we? Remember our discussion on the potential cost of losing a customer? So how do we strengthen this relationship, which wasn't easy to build in the first place? The answer is **feedback, feedback, feedback!**

> "CUSTOMER SERVICE IS JUST A DAY IN, DAY OUT ONGOING, NEVER ENDING, UNREMITTING, PERSEVERING, COMPASSIONATE, TYPE OF ACTIVITY."
>
> -LEON GORMAN

I can't emphasize enough how essential it is to establish a process that will allow us to receive customer feedback on an ongoing basis. The response we get from our customers helps us not only to improve where we lagged behind in providing exceptional customer service but also to change our course of direction to meet and exceed the new needs and ever changing expectations of our customers. There is more than one way to get customers' feedback, from paper-based comment cards to online-surveys. Electronic survey forms could be posted on the company's website or could also be distributed (and later collected) via email. Oftentimes, large organizations outsource this important job to companies that specialize in performing surveys in multiple mediums such as paper-based, over-the-phone, and electronically. No method is better than the other as long as it's affordable, timely, and works!

Regardless of the medium, to come up with an effective survey, your questions should revolve around the following three key elements: (1) How happy and satisfied are our customers with the use of our products or services? (2) What will we do different to better assist them? (3) Will they recommend us to their friends and family members?

Continue – Stop – Change – Start

Needless to say, if a feedback survey is not designed and delivered properly, it won't do any good to our business because then we will not know (a) what we are doing right and should

continue to do; (b) where we are going in the wrong direction and should **stop**; (c) where we need to **change** the way things are done; and finally, (d) what is it that we are supposed to be doing but haven't done so far and should **start**.

Surveys that work

We often come across surveys that are not only boring but also excessively lengthy, to the point that we simply don't think it's even worth our time to fill one out. So here are three quick tips to make your feedback surveys customer focused and attractive enough to get participation. (1) Keep them short and simple—it's a turn off for customers when they see a long and complex series of questions. (2) Make your surveys pertinent and timely; only ask questions that your customers can relate to at the time the survey is facilitated. (3) Offer some sort of incentive to customers for taking their precious time to help you improve your business, such as giving away a gift or a free entry for a prize draw. By the way, the complimentary item doesn't have to be pricey; you can be creative and offer a learning game or a book for kids. Parents, grandparents, aunts and uncles may choose to give away a few minutes in return for something that will bring joy and excitement for the children they love.

What to do with the feedback

Now that you've received feedback that addressed the key questions and targeted the right customer base, what do you do with it? All this time and effort will go in vain unless we take our customers' comments seriously and act upon them promptly! We should pay close attention to any patterns, i.e. several customers pointing to the same issue; but at the same time don't ignore any isolated instances either. Don't just assume that since the issue is raised by a single customer, the problem doesn't really exist. Perhaps this solo customer was the only one to bring this to your attention while others didn't even bother to report it. Even if the issue has impacted only one customer, can we afford to lose one customer? (Again: remember the discussion we had earlier regarding this.) Moreover,

> "STATISTICS SUGGEST THAT WHEN CUSTOMERS COMPLAIN, BUSINESS OWNERS AND MANAGERS OUGHT TO GET EXCITED ABOUT IT. THE COMPLAINING CUSTOMER REPRESENTS A HUGE OPPORTUNITY FOR MORE BUSINESS."
>
> -ZIG ZIGLAR

we should be conscious and aware of any elements of bias that may result if our survey gets filled out by a certain segment and not by all of our customers. What I mean by this is say you took a customer survey but only 25% of your customer base chose to participate. What if the ones who did participate were the ones who were unhappy with the service and wanted to complain? Such bias elements may result in having you doubt the things that you're even doing right. On the contrary, what if only the happy ones took their time to provide us with positive feedback while those who are dissatisfied considered taking the survey a waste of time and simply decided to take their business elsewhere? If so, won't you miss the areas of opportunities to improve? The key for a successful survey is to have it reach out to and filled out by a random customer base, to minimize the element of a bias. As a result, the feedback will provide a clear picture of where your relationship stands with your customer base; without it, you will not even know why you are losing business or where you are missing out on opportunities.

To wrap up, as time changes so do the *3P*—**(1) People (2) Priorities (3) Preferences.** The only way to track this change is to talk to our customers, by whatever means available to us and acceptable to them, and let them tell us how healthy our business relationship is and what else we can do, so it remains a lasting one! More importantly, take immediate actions every time we receive feedback in order to sustain our customer relationship.

Activity 13 – Your Survey, Your Questions

a) Come up with questions that you believe must be part of your survey.

b) Among the options of on-paper, over-the-phone, and electronic, which method will work best for your organization for conducting a survey and why?

c) Reflect on any of your personal preferences that may have changed within the last 10 years in terms of your purchasing habits or buying patterns.

Note: Please share your thoughts with others.

FINAL THOUGHTS

Customer Service 360 model is like a jigsaw puzzle, where every piece is essential; however, it's not until we put all the pieces together that we are able to see the *complete* picture. Likewise, each of the eight elements is essential to give our customers *complete* satisfaction that will result in **lasting loyalty and sustained profitability!**

If customer satisfaction is our number one priority then I'd say that *Customer Service Professionals* are our number one resource, who can help businesses achieve their goals by winning and keeping customers happy through delivering exceptional customer service. Management should acknowledge their contributions toward the success of the

> "WHETHER YOU ARE BIG OR SMALL, YOU CANNOT GIVE GOOD CUSTOMER SERVICE IF YOUR EMPLOYEES DON'T FEEL GOOD ABOUT COMING TO WORK."
>
> -MARTIN OLIVER

company. Remember what employees value most, even more than monetary compensation: a sense of appreciation.

If gaining new customers is tough, keeping them loyal is not effortless either. It is now up to you to apply the strategies laid out in this book to make it happen!

> "AS FAR AS CUSTOMERS ARE CONCERNED YOU ARE THE COMPANY. THIS IS NOT A BURDEN, BUT THE CORE OF YOUR JOB. YOU HOLD IN YOUR HANDS THE POWER TO KEEP CUSTOMERS COMING BACK — PERHAPS EVEN TO MAKE OR BREAK THE COMPANY."
>
> -UNKNOWN

Activity 14 – What did you learn?

We're almost done. Is there anything in this book that you think can be practically applied to bring benefit either to yourself, your company, or your customers?

Appendix One – 7%-38%-55% Rule

Ever heard of the 7%-38%-55% Rule? It's quite commonly discussed at business seminars. You may have attended a workshop on communications where they talked about the relative importance of *Words, Tone, and Body Language* in human communication, stating that (spoken) *words* count for only 7% of the message, *tone of voice* weighs 38% of the message, and our *body language* (facial expression and posture) makes up the remaining 55% (more than the other two factors combined). It's also known as *Mehrabian* rule as it comes out of the research done by Dr. Albert Mehrabian. This research is often misinterpreted, which results in misleading us as if our *words* do not carry as much weight in our communication. In other words, as long as one's tone and body language is positive, words don't matter much, which is totally opposite of what the *Mehrabian* rule is trying to imply. The rule applies *only* if we find inconsistency in the words, tone, and body language. For example, say you are interested in becoming a member of this golf club, so you go in and inquire about its membership procedure. The front desk person greets you in a dull and grumpy way and offers assistance by saying, *"What can I do for you?"* while texting on his cell phone (instead of establishing eye contact with you), and his facial expression clearly indicates that he cares not whether you join the club or not. Obviously, the words are *not* consistent with the tone and body language. According to *Mehrabian* rule, you'll give only 7% weight to what he actually said, *"What can I do for you?"* Instead the tone and body language will make up the remaining 83% of your impression of the club and the type of service they offer. By no means is the *Mehrabian* rule underestimating the importance of words, as if they don't mean much in comparison to tone and body language. Perhaps, most of us have experienced at one point or another in life that during a conversation, a single spoken word or phrase was enough to impact us emotionally, ruining the entire conversation, and at times even damaging relationships, business or personal. My point is that our choice of words carries a massive weight—they can either make or break it when it comes to building a rapport with our customers. In fact, words are as important (if not more) vis-à-vis the other two factors (tone and body language). Only where there is *inconsistency* between the words, tone, and the body language, is the relative importance of words significantly diminished as per the 7%-38%-55% Rule.

Appendix Two – Levels of Communication

No matter what business you are in and who your customers are, you must remain on top of the game when it comes to effective communications in order to provide extraordinary customer service. At any given point in time, you are communicating with the customer at one of the following three levels:

Level A: For centuries, communication at this level has taken place **face-to-face** where our Words, Tone, and Body Language (Facial Expression and Body Posture) all come into action when assisting our customers. This level of communication occurs at places like offices, retail stores, door-to-door sales etc. However, technology has opened new doors to assist customers at this level using live web-based video conferencing.

> "SPEND A LOT OF TIME TALKING TO CUSTOMERS FACE TO FACE. YOU'D BE AMAZED HOW MANY COMPANIES DON'T LISTEN TO THEIR CUSTOMERS."
>
> -ROSS PEROT

Level B: At this level we generally assist customers from a different location either over the **phone or via the Internet telephony** (aka VoIP - Voice over Internet Protocol) where we only use our Words and Tone. Since communication at this level is non-visual, non-verbal communication (facial expressions and body posture) is out of the picture. This level of communication occurs at places like call/contact centers (making outbound or receiving inbound calls) to address customers' concerns such as looking after their utility bills or checking up one's flight schedule.

> "TAKE THE TONE OF THE COMPANY THAT YOU ARE IN."
>
> -PHILLIP STRANHOPE

Advancement in telecommunication has not only made it possible but also affordable for companies to provide customer service off-shore and across continents. By the way, communication at this level doesn't have to take place hundreds or thousands of miles away from the customer. When calling the local pizza place for delivery or getting fries ordered at the drive-thru using the microphone, we're still communicating with only words and tone of voice.

Level C: At this level, the customer's interaction is neither face-to-face nor over the phone, so both Voice Tone and Non-Verbal clues are out of the game. At this level we primarily communicate to our

> "IN THE WORLD OF INTERNET CUSTOMER SERVICE, IT'S IMPORTANT TO REMEMBER YOUR COMPETITOR IS ONLY ONE MOUSE CLICK AWAY."
>
> -DOUG WARNER

customers by **Words in Writing**. Images, diagrams, and other visual illustrations are often used to complement our text—a picture is worth a thousand words. This includes any correspondence with customers via letters mailed through postal or courier service, email, online instant messaging (chat), text messaging, brochures, flyers, memos, manuals, websites, blogs (web logs), social media, and online bulletin boards. Regardless, you are providing information in both words and pictures to your customer.

Communication at any of the three levels (A, B, or C) can be equally effective and none is as such better than the other. However, given the situation, customers may prefer one level over another. If you like to take your friends out for dinner, you would prefer that your order is taken in person (Level A). However, to get your morning coffee during rush hour as you are late getting to work, you would prefer to use the drive-thru and place your order using the driveway microphone to save yourself some time (Level B). Whereas if you are planning a family vacation and like to check out the best hotel rates, perhaps, a good starting point would be to go to the Internet and compare different hotels online (Level C).

Long and short of it, no particular level (A, B, or C) takes precedence over the other. It's simply what is most suitable, convenient and preferable to the customer.

You can well imagine that oftentimes businesses, given the situation, choose to communicate with their customers at all three levels. For example, you plan to fly next month so you check out the airline website (Level C) to go through the flight schedules. Next, you prefer to speak to a live person as opposed to online booking, so you pick up the phone to make your reservation (Level B). Finally, during your flight, you enjoy the courteous and friendly customer service on board in person (Level A).

Activity 15 – Communicate at the "right" level

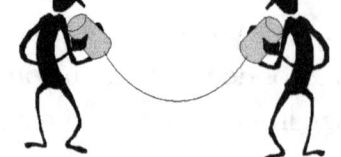

a) Which level of communication do you use to interact with most of your customers?

b) At which level is the most improvement needed to better assist the customers?

c) Can you think of a scenario where you'll need to communicate at all three levels (A, B, & C)?

Index

Notes

Notes

www.ingramcontent.com/pod-product-compliance
Lightning Source LLC
Chambersburg PA
CBHW081214170526
45165CB00009B/2818